Part of EA's world headquarters in
Redwood City, California.

EA: Celebrating 25 Years of Interactive Entertainment

Joe Funk: Author
Jason Hinman: Creative Director
John Gaudiosi: Associate Editor
Rob Jaskula: Associate Editor

Prima Games
A Division of Random House, Inc.
3000 Lava Ridge Court, Suite 100
Roseville, CA 95661

www.primagames.com

ISBN: 978-0-7615-5839-2
Library of Congress Catalog Card Number: 2007936225
Printed in the United States of America

08 09 10 11 LL 10 9 8 7 6 5 4 3 2 1

Without the help and support of the following people this book would not have been possible. Trudy Muller was pivotal in helping bring this entire project together. Mike Marsh added sizzle with his work on the companion DVD. Thanks also to Bing Gordon, Larry Probst, John Riccitiello, Trip Hawkins, Don Transeth, Greg Roensch, Nancy Smith, Frank Gibeau, Jeff Brown, Scott Cronce, Rich Hilleman, Jim Stadelman, Mike Marsh, Tammy Schachter, Debra Kempker, Andy Rolleri, Steve Schnur, Neil Young, Don Mattrick, David Gardner, Chip Lange, Nick Earl, Bryce Baer, Bryan Alvarez, David Grady, Peter Moore, Kathy Vrabeck and many others.

Introduction

In many ways, the birth and maturation of EA is the inspiration for me writing this book.

As a 15-year-old plunking away on my Apple II+ with 48K (plus a 16K expansion card to take it to a whopping 64K) and a first-gen gamer growing up in the heartland who was mesmerized by *PONG* at its inception; then Atari, then Intellivision, and all the others that followed, I was blown away when *One on One* came out. The game, the packaging, the "real" players – it was unlike anything I had ever seen before. Even from my distant vantage point, it just felt like these guys who called themselves "Electronic Arts" got it better than anyone else. 25 years later, after having the privilege of meeting the key people who made the company what it is today, it is clear they still do.

That experience helped propel me into a career that led to *Electronic Gaming Monthly* as an entry level editor in 1991, to become a co-founder of videogames.com, and to stay involved in the business ever since. Fast forward to now, and in the excitable words of a fellow Gen-Xer: "I'm a man. I'm a 40-year-old man!" And I'm still playing games.

Tom Brokaw and others refer to the generation who fought WWII as the greatest generation – no argument here – but I believe my generation, those of us around 40-years-old who were kids when videogames first exploded on the scene, may someday be referred to as the Gaming Generation. We're the ones who can remember a time (just barely) before there were electronic games, and in our fearless, early-adoptive mode of youth, embraced this new and riveting interactive past time which has forever changed the way we all think about entertainment.

When you leaf through this book, it's easy to see why: Many of the touchstones of pop culture that appealed to kids back then are present. What red-blooded American male growing up in the 1970s and 1980s wasn't fascinated by army men, sports, racing, dinosaurs and spies? But unlike every earlier generation, we didn't have to read a comic book or passively watch an experience on TV. For the first time, we could play along.

Who wouldn't want to not just be like Mike, but *be* Mike?; or fly a jet fighter; command or conquer an army; drive a Ferrari or Dale Earnhardt's #3; play (or beat) Tiger Woods; pop a wheelie; win a Stanley Cup; ride the half pipe; be coach, owner and GM of our favorite football team; kill orcs or Nazis; explore *The Simpons'* Springfield, or star in a rock band? And in an ironic twist, even emulate the Greatest Generation's greatest moment and storm the beaches of Normandy during D-Day?

And while videogames have gotten incredibly more realistic as we have grown older, a wonderful thing is happening: Games are broadening their demographic reach. It's not just about teenage boys anymore. My generation looks forward to the day when we will play games with our grandkids – maybe not the latest first-person shooter and its twitch-reflex requirements, but I'll man-up for a simple game of dodge ball with my future grandkids any day, and I know EA will be there enabling the possibilities.

This book is broken down into five, five-year chronological chunks of the company's history. In between these main chapters are related essays on Hollywood, music, casual games and *The Sims*; all of which demonstrate how after just 25 years, EA has risen to become a powerful force in 21st century pop culture. And with pixels getting smaller, the screens we play games on getting bigger, the sounds more surrounding, and even the man-machine interface getting more physical, the future of EA is even more exciting than its vibrant and colorful past.

Joe Funk
January, 2008

For further reading, outtakes, extend interviews and additional links, visit Prima.com.

Fans pack Times Square in New York City for the *Madden NFL 08* launch in August 2007.

Table of Contents

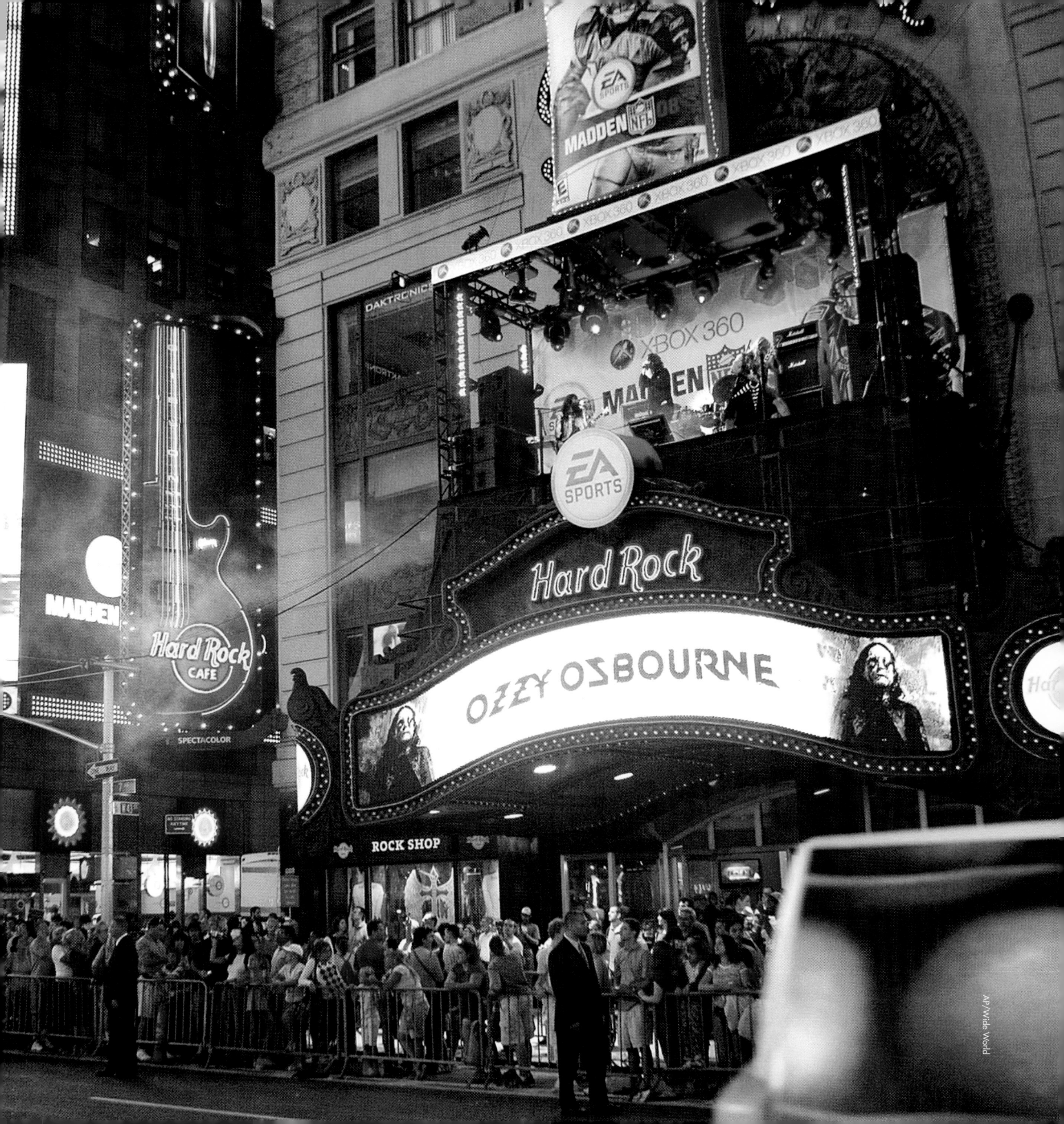

AP/Wide World

Foreword By Bing Gordon

Electronic Arts was founded on ideas.

We called software a new art form, and its creators were software artists. We believed that interactive was better than passive media, and that one day "software worthy of the minds that use it" would be more important than traditional media like films and television. "We see farther," we proclaimed, with faith that Moore's Law, the engine of Silicon Valley, would one day provide the power to put "real life in a box." We asked, "Can a computer make you cry?" and invited the new faithful to "Join us." We were oh, so young.

Twenty five years have passed, and many of the dreams have come true. Videogames are woven into the fabric of most young mens' lives, and increasingly popular with females and seniors. Game designers like Will Wright, Sid Meier, Shigeru Miyamoto, Sam Houser and John Carmack are renowned worldwide. Leading universities like Carnegie-Mellon, University of Southern California and University of British Columbia have pioneered successful degrees in game development. Our own children think we're cool, at least temporarily, if our latest games are good enough for their friends to come over and play.

In short, videogames, once considered a passing fad by experts at leading news journals, have earned respect.

It took a decade after our original 1982 business plan vision of "interactive as a mass market" for me to experience what "mass" actually meant. I was carrying an EA SPORTS-logo'd gym bag to a magazine interview in New York City and jumped into a cab. Before I could give the driver an address, he looked back at me, and in his gritty Brooklyn accent intoned, "EA SPORTS. It's in da game!" Videogames had reached the tipping point, for me at least, when that Yellow Cab driver crossed the chasm.

Another "we have arrived moment" occurred while beta testing *The Sims* over Christmas, 1999. My two daughters and their friends were smitten, scrunched over the PC monitor two-to-a-chair, taking turns and playing for 15 minutes each. It was fascinating and heart-warming to watch, but at length, I was burned out. Imagine my surprise when, moments later from the next room, I heard the kind of blood-curdling scream of pain that every parent fears. As I rushed into the computer room, my 8-year old daughter Allegra leapt into my arms, screaming in agony, "She killed my Mommy!" It took several minutes to figure out that her friend's female Sim, tired of her flirtations being interrupted, had lured my daughter's "Mommy" Sim into the bathroom and bricked the door closed until she turned into a tombstone. Yes, I thought, a computer can "make you cry."

It has taken several generations of "founders" to build Electronic Arts. There were about 20 of us in EA's first warehouse, where we shipped out our first games in May, 1983 including *Archon, Pinball Construction Set, M.U.L.E.*, and *Hard Hat Mack*. Another group of "founders" made the treacherous transition to console videogames in the late 1980's, after secretly "reverse engineering" the Sega Genesis system, and launching games such as *John Madden Football, Lakers vs Celtics*, and *Budokan* in 1990. Then there were "founders" who launched EA Europe out of a London hotel in the mid-80's with *Populous*, and more "founders" who re-invented EA Canada in Vancouver the mid-90's with *FIFA* and *Need for Speed*. Origin Systemscame along in the mid-90's with *Ultima Online, EA Maxis* arrived in the late-90's with *The Sims, EA Pogo* hit in the early 2000's with *Club Pogo*, and even more resourceful "founders" who built EA's publishing businesses in more than 40 countries.

It has taken a village of entrepreneurs to build Electronic Arts.

We faced so many nay-sayers and unbelievers along the way. EA's founding board of directors told us in 1983, 10 years before

CAN A COMPUTER MAKE YOU CRY?

Right now, no one knows. This is partly because many would consider the very idea frivolous. But it's also because whoever successfully answers this question must first have answered several others.

Why do we cry? Why do we laugh, or love, or smile? What are the touchstones of our emotions?

Until now, the people who asked such questions tended not to be the same people who ran software companies. Instead, they were writers, filmmakers, painters, musicians. They were, in the traditional sense, artists.

We're about to change that tradition. The name of our company is Electronic Arts.

SOFTWARE WORTHY OF THE MINDS THAT USE IT.

We are a new association of electronic artists united by a common goal — to fulfill the enormous potential of the personal computer.

In the short term, this means transcending its present use as a facilitator of unimaginative tasks and a medium for blasting aliens. In the long term, however, we can expect a great deal more.

These are wondrous machines we have created, and in them can be seen a bit of their makers. It is as if we had invested them with the image of our minds. And through them, we are learning more and more about ourselves.

We learn, for instance, that we are more entertained by the involvement of our imaginations than by passive viewing and listening. We learn that we are better taught by experience than by memorization. And we learn that the traditional distinctions — the ones that are made between art and entertainment and education — don't always apply.

TOWARD A LANGUAGE OF DREAMS.

In short, we are finding that the computer can be more than just a processor of data.

It is a communications medium: an interactive tool that can bring people's thoughts and feelings closer together, perhaps closer than ever before. And while fifty years from now, its creation may seem no more important than the advent of motion pictures or television, there is a chance it will mean something more.

Something along the lines of a universal language of ideas and emotions. Something like a smile.

The first publications of Electronic Arts are now available. We suspect you'll be hearing a lot about them. Some of them are games like you've never seen before, that get more out of your computer than other games ever have. Others are harder to categorize — and we like that.

WATCH US.

We're providing a special environment for talented, independent software artists. It's a supportive environment, in which big ideas are given room to grow. And some of America's most respected software artists are beginning to take notice.

We think our current work reflects this very special commitment. And though we are few in number today and apart from the mainstream of the mass software marketplace, we are confident that both time and vision are on our side.

Join us.

We see farther.

EA ELECTRONIC ARTS™

EA SPORTS was launched, to stop trying to create an EA brand, because, "You can't brand media." Our retailer partners told us not to bother with *The Sims* ("People games don't sell!"), not to sequel *Madden Football* ("No one buys sports games twice"), and not to charge subscription fees for *Ultima Online* service ("No one will pay for an MMO!"). After Atari cratered in 1982-83, there were years of articles on the death of videogames, and one computer manufacturer CEO proclaimed in the late 1980s that there was "no home computer market."

Our passionate group of videogamers who saw farther, however, persevered.

Yet there is still much to be done. The next generation of always online players expect their interactive entertainment to offer clickable depth, persistent personas and reputations, user-generated content, social graph connections, newsfeeds, tags, and scalable graphics from JPEGs to 1080p digital movies. The future of gaming depends on new generations of inventors who can also "See Farther."

May you find, in this time vault of videogaming, your favorite years, your best teams, your fondest frags, your most-uploaded cities and avatars, and your most successful "money play." Perhaps you'll come across a game that got you through a hard year of adolescence or a dull year of college Physics, bad health, or a too-quiet holiday. Maybe it was even a game where you met your significant other or new best friend.

When EA founders asked gamers to "Join Us," we were inviting YOU.

What a ride this has been!

Thanks for playing.

Bing Gordon • Chief Creative Officer
Electronic Arts • 1982-????

Years I-V: Manifesto
Molding a New Media with a Mission

With nearly $3 billion in revenues for 2006 and 7,200 employees across the globe, it's hard to believe the humble roots that Electronic Arts came from in 1982 helped form the world's largest third-party interactive software developer and household name today.

But one cannot document the history of EA, without first telling a brief history of videogames.

In the early 1970s, the groundbreaking *PONG* videogame propelled Atari into being the fastest growing company in the United States. *PONG* was housed in a cabinet about the size of a phone booth, was played entirely on a video screen anchored inside, and was placed alongside more traditional games like pinball machines in the dark and smoky arcades of the time.

PONG wasn't the first videogame. It wasn't even an immediate smash. But eventually it caught on enough to become commercially successful and its crude, low-res graphics left an indelible pixel and served as an important catalyst for a revolution that would change the way we think of entertainment.

The machines sold well enough to convince Atari that building a videogame console for homes could be a financial success and they poured money into developing a cartridge-based videogame system called the Atari 2600.

From the start, Atari would control all aspects of game development, from hardware development and manufacturing through game design and distribution. In fact, Atari was the sole supplier of software for their system for many years after the 2600 hit the market.

All of this would change in 1979. Several Atari game developers had become fed up with a culture that relegated them to bit players in the production of a videogame. Getting no credit and no royalties was seen as an injustice that would not stand. With that, programmers representing more than half of all Atari game revenue decided to leave and stake out their future with a firm they called "Activision".

Atari sued to maintain control of all software development, lost the case when the courts finally handed down its decision in 1982, and third-party developers flourished.

By the time the court cases had finally been settled, over 100 small gaming firms had been set up to cater to the burgeoning market. With third-party development and distribution now a reality, new companies

The name Electronic Arts came from management's belief that game makers were truly software artists.

were seemingly springing up every week. Game designers and developers were at the center of these new firms, and they were able to recruit talented programming staffs.

This new market caught the eye of a young developer named Trip Hawkins who was working at Apple in 1982. Thanks to a $2 million venture capital investment through Don Valentine, Hawkins was able to start his computer software firm, Amazin' Software. Valentine even allowed Amazin' to use its offices until the company established itself. After the incorporation of Amazin' Software on May 28, 1982, Hawkins would fund the company himself until the end of the year.

While Hawkins plugged away on the business plan while waiting to close on the venture capital, he realized he could look to old friends for help. The company's first hires in August included Rich Melmon, Dave Evans, Bing Gordon, and Pat Marriott. Thanks to the capital investments, the small company was able to move into its own offices with 11 employees by the end of 1982.

PONG made Atari the fastest growing company in the United States, but by the 1980s their stranglehold on the videogame market was loosening.

Originally calling for "computer software that would make a personal computer worth owning," EA staked out its future plans in its 1982 business plan. The plan called for a six-year growth period, at the end of which EA would be a billion-dollar company. Certainly these were high expectations for a firm that was only the 136th-largest software manufacturer in 1982, but the EA team was not swayed.

Larry Probst, who has been with the company since 1984 and was CEO from 1991-2007, cites the intensely competitive attitude of the company in its formative years as a contributing force.

"Second just doesn't feel very good around here," he said. "I think that's had a lot to do with why the company has been successful over a long period of time and why it continues to be the market leader."

After Amazin' Software was found on May 28, things moved swiftly. Thanks to help from Melmon, the business plan was finished and the company was poised to start developing and publishing games. The company quickly outgrew its space in Valentine's offices and then outgrew space in Burlingame, California, before settling in Silicon Valley. While it continued to add

AP/Wide World

Atari's 2600 was the top dog in the gaming world, but a restrictive set of rules for game publishing made EA steer clear of the system.

a name: Electronic Arts. It was made official in October.

The company began to license software to publish in earnest, with the hope of having games out in the spring of 1983. At this point, the EA brass had a decision to make—develop titles for the expanding home computer market where Apple was poised to dominate, or for the current top dog of videogame consoles, Atari, with their 2600 system and soon-to-be-released 5200.

But EA soon recognized that Atari's game development philosophy went against its core principles. Not only did Atari rely heavily on in-house game development; they actively sought to stop production by companies such as Activision, by now the largest third-party developer. Additionally, Atari paid its game developers a one-time fee per game and then assumed ownership; they would not allow for a programmer's name to appear in the credits of a game, let alone on a box. Developers for Atari's system were also not paid royalties based on sales of the games they created and at the end of the day, their hard work was largely unrecognized and underappreciated. After careful consideration, EA decided to not publish games for Atari's home consoles.

That's not to say that EA didn't publish games for Atari hardware. In fact, the first EA games shipped for only two platforms—the Apple II and Atari's 800-series home computers. The decision to not publish games for Atari's home consoles would, in fact, save the company from near certain ruin in late 1983 and 1984.

With the decision made to begin by supporting the Apple II and Atari 800 platforms,

new hires dedicated to its philosophy of programmers-as-artists, a big hurdle soon popped up: the name of the company.

Throughout 1982, several employees expressed dissatisfaction with the name of the firm, though not the concept behind it. Several late-night brainstorming sessions yielded possibilities such as SoftArt and Electronic Artists. These names were rejected for sounding too much like another software company (Software Artists) and for not reflecting the true nature of the company (it was argued that the programmers were the artists, and EA was simply the publisher). After vigorous debate, they finally settled on

"It was from the experience of working with the software geniuses at Apple... that I realized the best software engineers are artists, and they have the ego and the temperament and the genius of great artists, and they need to be managed that way, and that's really interesting." —Trip Hawkins

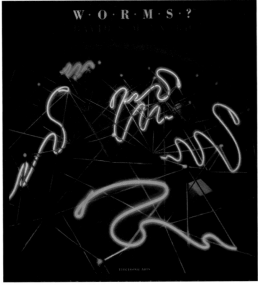

(top) The Apple II's success brought the reality of personal computers into millions of homes during the 1980's. (bottom) *Worms?* shipped as part of EA's initial launch in May, 1983.

the EA team set about to finding programmers and games to publish under their new banner. To accomplish this, they recruited what were considered some of the best independent game designers in the industry, including Bill Budge, Free Fall Associates, and Ozark Softscape. They were given the title of "software artists" to reflect their contributions to individual products. EA would give the artists not only full, frontal credit for their work, but royalties as well. This innovative strategy allowed EA to attract top-notch game artists right from the start, a tradition that carries on to this day.

The company also made a commitment to embrace cutting-edge technology from the beginning—eschewing then-standard cassettes and cartridges for floppy disks (a format supported by both the Atari 800 and Apple II).

In addition to using the latest technology, EA decided to take a new approach to packaging as well. Each game would be shipped in a square box, featuring not only the game title, but also the programmer's name and flashy cover art. With each developer becoming an "artist," it seemed only natural that covers looked like the latest rock album covers as well, a style later copied by many other software companies.

With the company hurtling toward game production, a new problem arose. In the original EA business plan, the company had made it a goal of distributing its products directly to retailers who would sell the games to end users. At the time, every major software firm—including giants like Microsoft—used outside distributors to sell its software. EA wanted nothing to do with

this practice and sought to force retailers to buy games directly from EA or not purchase them at all, a brazen move for a company that had yet to publish. In fact, many competitors told friends of EA that without outside distribution, the company would go belly-up in under a year.

With programmer talent on board and a sales strategy in place, it was time for EA to sink or swim in the spring of 1983. All 20-some employees crammed into the warehouse in May to pack boxes with the first batch of games ready to ship. Bing Gordon recalls the day well: "I think we had about 22 employees by then, and we all went to the warehouse, and we all stuffed boxes. And I'm sure the three full-timers in the warehouse were driven crazy by how inefficient we were, but also how exuberant. It was pretty exciting to finally be shipping the games we'd been working on for so long."

The launch titles for EA were *Hard Hat Mack, Archon, Pinball Construction Set, Worms?,* and *M.U.L.E.*, with *Hard Hat Mack* considered the official "first game" for EA. The employees revealed in launching their first titles and saw nothing but success ahead. *Axis Assassin, The Last Gladiator,* and *Murder on the Zinderneuf* also shipped in the next few months.

The launch titles were not just done by some of the best game artists in the world, but also broke new ground in the industry. Budge's *Pinball Construction Set* pioneered the "builder" genre of games, and spawned three immediate sequels published by EA. The game would go on to sell 300,000 copies, EA's first commercial hit.

Not only was *Pinball Construction Set* a success on the shelves, but to EA, it symbolized

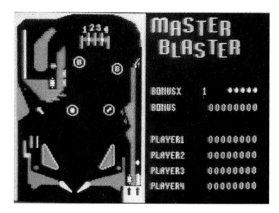

Budge's Pinball Construction Set pioneered the builder genre while showcasing EA's album-style artwork at the same time.

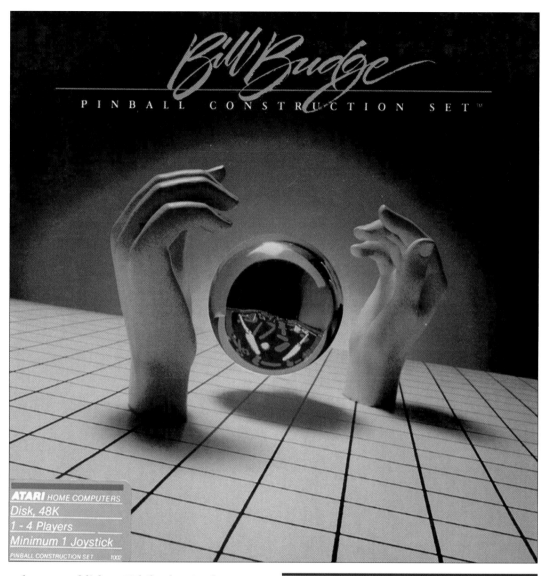

what a game should be. It was fun to play and allowed gamers to do something constructive with their brains instead of doing something passive like watching television.

Pinball Construction Set wasn't the only groundbreaking game from EA at launch. *M.U.L.E*, developed by Dan Bunten of Ozark Softscape, is considered to be revolutionary in that it became the first game to successfully execute a four-player multiplayer game on one machine. Developed well ahead of its time, the colony-in-space commerce simulation that is *M.U.L.E.* consistently finds itself on Best Games of All-Time lists. *M.U.L.E's* popularity even extends to the present. One big fan is Nancy Smith, who has been with the company since 1984 and now runs *The Sims* Label: "I love *M.U.L.E*. Still to this day, I think it's a great game."

Through the spring and summer of 1983, the outlook was not so rosy for the fledgling

software publisher. While the Apple II was on its way to becoming a fixture in homes and schools around the country, the Atari 800 computer never took off as anticipated. Of the first five games that EA shipped, only two were Apple II compatible, while all five were developed for the 800.

Fighting for survival, EA saw a future with

"And with *Pinball Construction Set*, yeah, it's a pinball machine, but you're talking about one of the first examples of user-generated content, and the creativity of creating your own game and feeling empowered by that." —Trip Hawkins

300,000

Number of copies *Pinball Construction Set* sold in 1983, making it EA's first commercial hit.

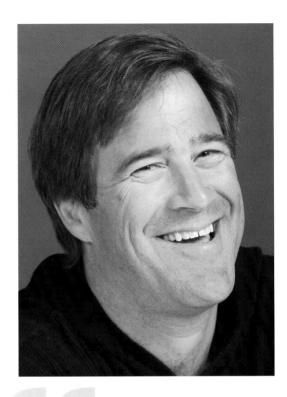

the fast-growing Commodore 64 platform just as Atari and the videogame console market was starting to implode. Too many subpar games had flooded the market and jaded consumers, with many dismissing videogames as just another passing fad. With the 1983 holiday season fast approaching, EA managed to port five of its games successfully to the Commodore in time for Thanksgiving, assuring the company of holiday sales and the revenue to stay afloat.

Wizard, the first EA game developed solely for the Commodore 64, included a new feature that is a hallmark of many games today—a level editor. While not customizable to the depth of the later *Adventure Construction Set*, gamers were permitted a chance to create their own levels in the game. Although limited by several issues, including not being able to add magic to levels, the rudimentary level editor would come into its own in 1985.

Another game released in late 1983 would prove to be revolutionary as well. *One on One* would set EA SPORTS on a path that has made it an icon in popular culture. In *One on One*, consumers saw real-life sports legends attached to a game and appearing as themselves for the first time.

Revolutionary gameplay (and a janitor to clean up broken glass after thunderous dunks) showed that *One on One* was a pioneer sports game. Its animation, although limited to two characters, was surprisingly detailed for its era. The game proved so successful on the Apple II that it was soon ported to the Commodore 64, Amiga, and even the Atari 7800 console.

Not only was it popular on its own accord,

it spawned a sequel: 1988's *Jordan vs. Bird*. This game would set a precedent for EA Sports updating their sports franchises that we still see today. EA also saw a broader opportunity with the release of *One on One*. They envisioned a series of sports titles starring real athletes and teams playing in simulations that were as authentic as current technology would allow. The formula also called for signing an engaging personality from the respective sport to help them promote the game.

In early 1984, EA turned to developer Robin Antonick to explore the feasibility of making an 11-on-11 football simulation for the Apple II, and began the search for a personality in football that it could market similar to Julius Erving or Larry Bird. Being based in the Bay area, a former coach-turned-broadcaster caught their attention—the affable and legendary John Madden—and the company set about securing rights to the project. It would take a few more years for this dream to become reality, but the game plan was now in place.

As 1984 unfolded, the Videogame Crash was having a devastating effect. While sales flagged for home-based videogame consoles, Atari and other manufacturers were pumping a glut of inferior software into the market and consumers quit buying games. Not only did this strategy fail, but it turned many consumers off to gaming, polluted the market for the survivors, and retarded industry growth. As the console makers like Atari collapsed, they took many software companies, big and small, down with them. The industry shakeout would last deep into 1984, with the direct effects felt until 1987, and some effects

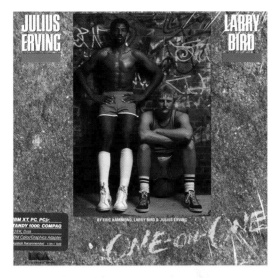

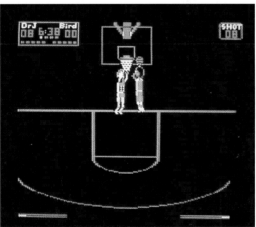

(left) Dr. J and Larry Bird helped catapult the NBA to new heights in the 1980s. (above) *One on One* is the forerunner of today's EA Sports offerings and a direct predecessor of *NBA Live*.

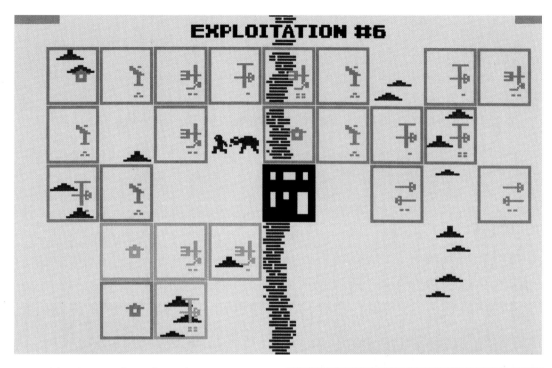

EXPLOITATION #6

(above) Despite the crude graphics, *M.U.L.E.* was revolutionary for its ingenious game design.

(right) The arrival of Larry Probst marked the beginning of an important era for EA.

"The first six months were pretty challenging. The business wasn't in great shape. We were really scraping and scrambling to generate revenue... and in short order, we decided to completely change our distribution strategy, build our own sales force, and change our pricing structure"
-Larry Probst

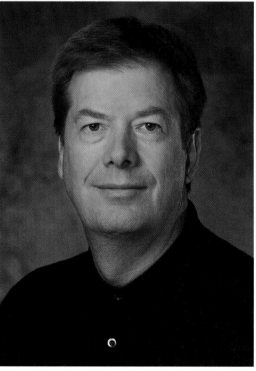

lasting well into the 1990s. The Crash pushed back the goals of the original EA business plan—it would take 11 more years for EA to become a billion-dollar company.

1984 saw a first for EA in gaming: its first sequel. The 1983 hit *Pinball Construction Set* was so popular that gamers were clamoring for more. Developer Will Harvey had first designed *Music Construction Set* as a music builder when he was just 15 years old, and two years later he was approached by EA to publish his game, which really wasn't even a game in the traditional sense. With help from EA in refining his title, its release was eagerly anticipated.

Music Construction Set wasn't even originally designed to be released on its own. Harvey had initially built the program to make music for his 1982 release, Lancaster. With EA on board, Harvey polished the program into an interface for computer enthusiasts while EA put the *Construction Set* name on it, viewing it as a thematic successor to *Pinball Construction Set*.

With high hopes, the game shipped. It would go on to be released, in various forms, to the Apple II, Apple IIgs, Amiga, and IBM PC. The IBM-compatible version broke some new technological ground as well by using a cassette tape drive where gamers could record their *Music Construction Set* compositions and play them on their home stereos.

Not only was *Music Construction Set* a big hit for the time, it was a success by any of today's benchmarks. It would go on to sell over 1 million copies, the first EA game to do so.

With his name on the packaging, Harvey became a celebrity in the gaming world at just 17. He would go on to develop several other games for EA throughout the 1980s.

1984 saw another significant release by Dan Bunten and Ozark Softscape. *Seven Cities of Gold* was a pioneering game that showcased Bunten's imagination and skill as a game developer. Showing that *M.U.L.E.* was anything but a fluke, Bunten defined the genre of historical gaming that would later be seen in games like *Oregon Trail* and *Civilization*. In *Seven Cities*, players took on the role of a 15th Century Spanish explorer who sails to the New World. After setting up missions and forts, the player then had the option of conquering or peacefully trading with the natives.

Throughout the company's first few years, a trend in quality game design became apparent. Several important and innovative games were released by EA, impressive considering the modest size of the company, and it would continue to augment its reputation as a destination for game developers in a trend that would only continue as the years went on. It is a notable accomplishment that EA's idea of recognizing game developers as artists was not just a noble philosophy, but a highly lucrative reality.

While software companies across North America were shutting down in 1983 and 1984, EA was bringing in the talent that would lead the company well into the 21st Century. Larry Probst, a young executive at rival Activision, had some experience in the gaming industry, but was still an up-and-comer. He had studied business administration at the University of Delaware and had spent time working with Clorox and Johnson & Johnson. When EA hired him away from Activision, he became the firm's

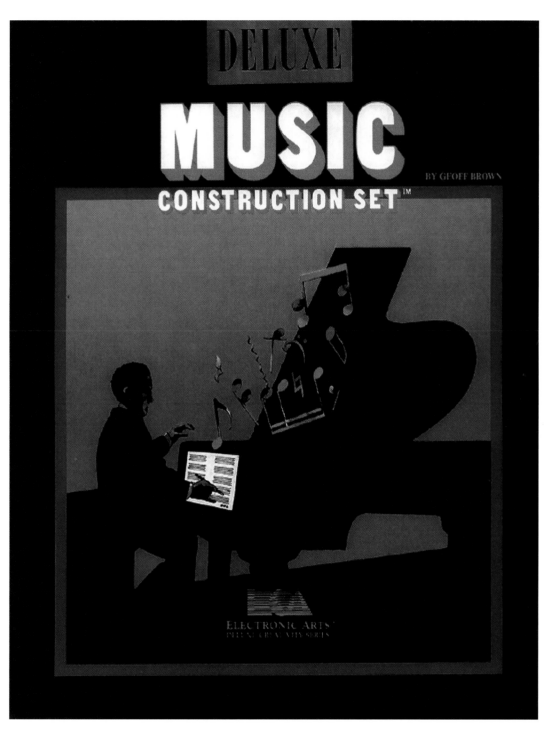

Music Construction Set came about as an accident: it was a program used to compose music for other games.

EA was worth $8 million in 1984, a far cry from where Hawkins wanted it to be, but at least it was surviving a turbulent videogame market.

vice president of sales—the first of many hats he would wear over the next two decades. Few could imagine that when Probst arrived in 1984 that a 50-man company with all of $8 million dollars in revenue would become the pop cultural powerhouse that it is today.

As the sun set on an eventful 1984, it was evident that 1985 would be another big year for EA. With Probst on board for his first full year, more success was expected from the

small software company with big goals. Both 1985 and 1986 would see those goals start to become reality, while a large Japanese monster was poised to stomp across the Pacific Ocean and into American homes.

In Japan, Nintendo had been having commercial success since 1983 with its Family Computer, otherwise known as the Famicom. When Nintendo decided to bring its machine stateside for 1985, the company looked to Atari to distribute the Famicom in the American market. When the deal with Atari fell through, Nintendo decided to import its renamed Nintendo Entertainment System on its own through a small Washington-based office.

Although EA explored the possibility of developing games for the upstart system, a five game per-year limit that Nintendo imposed on its third-party developers helped keep EA away from the console market for the time being. While EA would continue to see success in the home-computer market, Nintendo would quickly begin to dominate the home-console arena. Probst remembers the decision to not publish games for the NES well.

"We essentially ignored the 8-bit Nintendo business. I remember Mr. Arakawa and Howard Lincoln coming to EA in 1984 and 1985 and pitching us on support for the 8-bit Nintendo system, and Trip would have no part of it."

For EA, 1985 saw two more titles in the popular *Construction Set* line of games. Don Daglow's *Adventure Construction Set* allowed gamers their first opportunity to create their own "adventure" game. The graphics designer of the game gave gamers the chance to set their own stories and adventures and share them with friends. The title included a pre-made game and an option to randomize, and later edit, the features of a randomized game.

Adventure Construction Set was so influential it earned a SPA Gold Disk Award and spawned an EA contest for user-generated content that was to be judged by its own game testers. The winning games were further refined by EA and released as a collection for fans of *Adventure Construction Set*. The

developers were even paid royalties for their creations. Not only was *Adventure Construction Set* popular in its own day, it influenced several other games of its genre. In fact, level editors that are present in many of today's games owe a debt to *Adventure Construction Set* and *Wizard*.

The second game in the *Construction Set* line to come out that year didn't share its name with its predecessors. When Rick Koenig's *Racing Destruction Set* hit the market in 1985, it seemed to be a big departure from previous games in the series. *Racing Destruction Set*

Nintendo was slowly taking over the Asian game market with the Famicom while preparing for a U.S. launch, but a five game annual limit imposed on software developers caused EA to steer clear of the system.

"Our goal was to be a premium brand, start small and then build from a base. And we had learned in the advertising world about how to create a quality brand. Some of the tricks were to let users discover you, and also to seem a little bit zany. We believed – and we've done this in advertising – that if you seem a little bit illogical and crazily committed to whatever you're doing, potential customers take that as one indication of intent to quality. We'd all read *Zen and the Art of Motorcycle Maintenance*, where Pirsig talks about intent to quality.

So we combined those two things getting across intent to quality, because the way the big companies would do it is they'd say, "Quality is job 1," but then spend $100 million in advertising, and every consumer knows that that's foretelling of quality that is not job 1.

So we tried to figure that out and make it feel like missionary zeal." —Bing Gordon

allowed games to take several different modes of transportation and race against either computer opponents or against a friend in split-screen action. Where the game really stood out, however, was in its track editor. Like many racing games after it, *RDS* allowed gamers to customize tracks in many imaginative ways. Using templates to start, gamers could then insert ramps and other obstacles and even change the terrain characteristics of the track; it was the first racing game to allow that level of customization.

Another 1985 release almost never made it to store shelves: Don Daglow had been working on a monster-themed combat game for several months with a design team, but couldn't come up with a name that would survive a copyright search. In a crunch to meet the package-design deadline, Daglow turned to marketing director Bing Gordon for advice. Gordon thought the name should be both amusing and reflect the nature of the game and came up with *Mail Order Monsters*.

The game would prove to be yet another hit for EA. Praised for its innovative cooperative play features, *Mail Order Monsters* allowed gamers to create their own beasts and either do battle with each other or team up with friends to take on the computer in combat or capture the flag modes. Not only were the monsters customizable and fluid in their attributes, gamers could independently save their monsters onto diskettes to play later with friends on their machines.

Daglow, a former director of game development with Mattel's Intellivision, had come to EA after the videogame crash in 1983. He quickly built on his reputation as an influential game designer with Electronic

Arts, and 1986 would be his biggest year with the company.

The first of Daglow's games to be released in 1986 was *Thomas M. Disch's Amnesia*, built on a story by the popular science-fiction author. Waking up one morning with no recollection of the events that have led him to become both engaged and wanted for murder, the hero of the game must unravel the events of his life. Featuring over 4,000 actual locations in New York City, the captivating, well-written, and very difficult text-based sim was one of the most popular text games of the 1980s.

Daglow followed with several other games throughout 1986. *Lords of Conquest* featured a *Risk*-style world domination game. It later earned awards in a retrospective as one of the best games of its era. *Super Boulder Dash* was an entertaining sequel to the original *Boulder Dash*, bringing back the popular character Rockford and his cave-digging adventures.

Despite his commercial successes with games he developed and programmed in 1986, it was a game that Daglow produced that would be his most important title of the year. *World Tour Golf*, programmed by Evan and Nicky Robinson, featured not only a full-featured golf game, but included a course editor as well. Designed with the intent of having a golf game for home computers to compete with the Nintendo Entertainment System's *Nintendo Golf*, *World Tour Golf* broke new ground in the sporting game world.

Featuring a course editor that (for the time) allowed for extraordinarily detailed courses, players could take several avenues: They could accurately re-create their home-

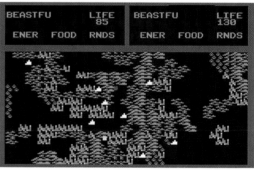

Don Daglow's *Mail Order Monsters* got its name only after a copyright search eliminated all of his original ideas for the game's title.

For the time, *World Tour Golf* had world-class graphics and depth.

town or favorite course, build up famous courses around the world, or create fantasy courses with details that had never been seen in a game before that time. After seeing the success of their *Mail Order Monsters* in 1985, the Robinsons and Don Daglow had high expectations for their golf title. Sales did not disappoint, and the game was awarded an SPA Gold Disk for its commercial success.

While *World Tour Golf* was a commercial success and featured an innovative course editor as well, the lasting legacy of the game is more what it symbolized than the game itself. Electronic Arts had not released a true sports title since 1983's *One on One*, and the company had little time or energy devoted to the sports market. *World Tour Golf* would lead directly to EA's *Jordan Versus Bird* and successful *Earl Weaver Baseball* line, and more importantly provide a link from *One on One* to EA's later sports titles. In a way, *World Tour Golf* helped to spawn the line of games that would one day become EA Sports. For the time being, it certainly jolted EA into considering more sports titles.

More success would follow for EA in 1986. Will Harvey's *Marble Madness* was not only revolutionary for its gameplay and level design; it was one of the most popular arcade games of the mid-1980s. Its original arcade version was the first arcade game to feature stereo sound.

As EA's first five years came to a close in 1986, the future looked bright. Though the company had not met its fiscal goal of being a billion-dollar firm—that would still have to wait several years—Electronic Arts had quickly established itself as an innovative industry leader.

Not only was *Music Construction Set* a big hit for the time, it was a success by any benchmark of today. It would go on to sell over one million copies.

1,000,000

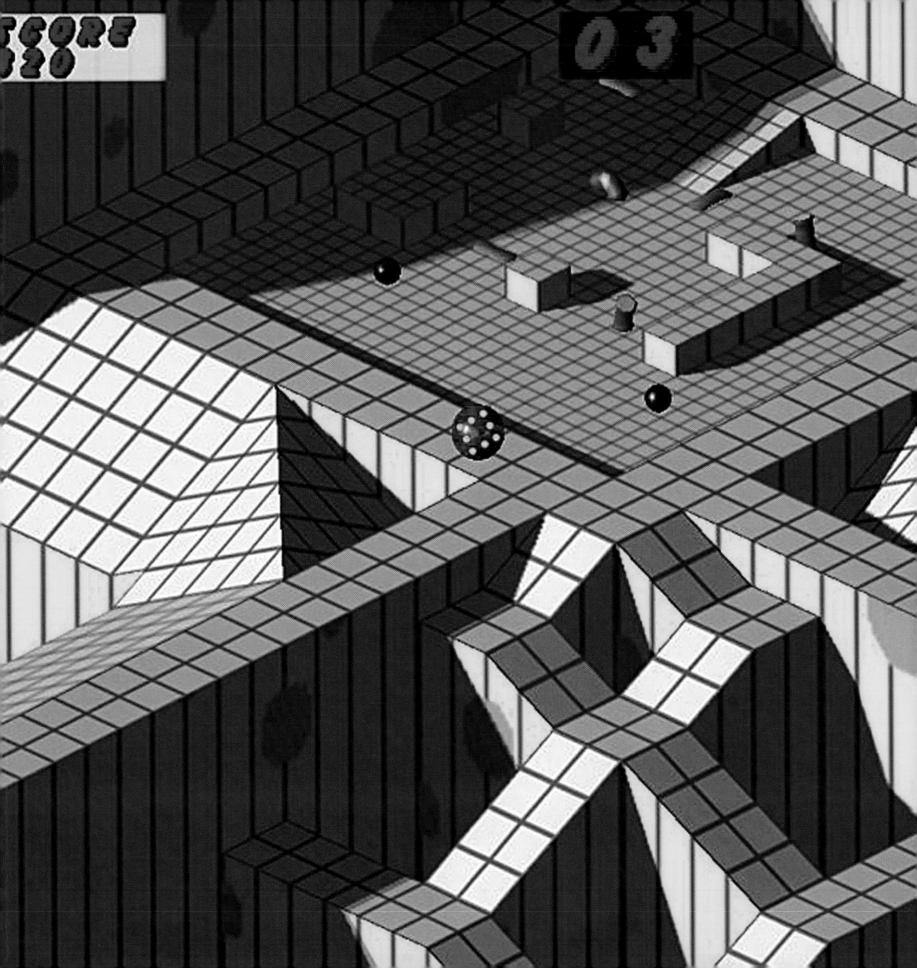

MARBLE MADNESS

APPLE IIe, IIc
128K, 1 or 2 players
Joystick recomm'd
Color Monitor recomm'd

MARBLE MADNESS

ELECTRONIC ARTS

SCORE
390

By 1987 Electronic Arts had established itself as a respected game publisher.

Looking back at the first five years of the company, there are several reasons for this: By only publishing games for computer platforms, EA managed to avoid the monopolistic policies of the console manufacturers, first Atari and then Nintendo. Not having creative restrictions on the content or quantity or their games had allowed EA to publish the games they wanted when they wanted to publish them. Although entering the console-gaming market would become a necessity for EA, the company had managed to carve a niche for itself in the home-computer game market that was not insignificant by the end of its first five years.

A second reason for the fast rise of the company was its treatment of game developers. No longer were anonymous programmers hacking away in a dark corner—EA brought the designer to the forefront. The fresh concept of giving programmers credit and royalties for their work allowed EA to attract quality individuals like Bill Budge, Don Daglow, and Will Harvey from the very start. Collaborative efforts were undertaken for the first time by design teams, making game design a group project.

Engaging in these sweeping reforms from the beginning proved to be a risk well-taken for Electronic Arts. In being able to release fun, well-received games from its first batch in May 1983, EA set a tone for quality that would permeate throughout the rest of the decade.

In regards to the executive leadership of Hawkins, Probst and Gordon, the first stanza of the company had to be viewed as a success as well. EA had innovative product lines being developed by top-notch programmers, forward-thinking business and marketing straegies. Not only had the company survived the Videogame Crash in 1983, but business was actually thriving.

In five years, EA had become a videogame industry innovator and leader. Although the genesis of the company was successful in its own right, it would be on another Genesis that EA would come into its own.

"It started on the Genesis," Probst said. That moved us into the mainstream business and we really started to build a company from that point forward." ●

(opposite) EA's original electronic artists from the 1983 ad include (left to right) Top: Mike Abbott (*Hard Hat Mack*), Dan Bunten (*M.U.L.E.*), Jon Freeman (*Archon* designer), Anne Westfall (*Archon* programmer), Bill Budge (*Pinball Construction Set*) Bottom: Matt Alexander (*Hard Hat Mack*), John Fields (*Axis Assassin*), David Maynard (*Worms?*).

The Sims Spawns a New Way to Play

Perhaps no game has quite captured the spirit of the modern videogame community quite like *The Sims*. The great irony of its success of what many people thought was a project that would never see the light of day, and originally involved no people, has come to be viewed as a Will Wright masterpiece. In the end, clearer heads would prevail, and today *The Sims*, its sequel, and its expansions have sold over 95 million copies the world over.

Like many of today's greatest game franchises, *The Sims* came from humble beginnings. Developer Will Wright had been publishing games with EA and other companies since he was just 17, and was already considered an innovative mind in game development. Affiliated with Maxis during the mid-1990s, the company developed titles such as the hit *SimCity* series and other spin-offs including *SimSafari*. In 1997, the studio was purchased by EA.

Former Electronic Arts CEO Larry Probst offered this anecdote about the acquisition and Wright's latest project.

"We were really fortunate because Maxis had *SimCity* and when we started the due diligence we asked, 'What's going on with Will Wright?' Their response was, 'He's

working offsite with six or seven people on an architectural design tool.' It turned out he was in an office literally next door to where EA was located."

After seeking out Wright the acquisition would become a no-brainer. "They started talking and kicking around some creative ideas and that was the beginning of *The Sims*. We ended up acquiring Maxis, hiring Will, getting *The Sims* and the rest is history," recalls Probst.

Before the acquisition, Wright had been working with a team on a project codenamed *Dollhouse*. "The project got started before EA acquired us," he recalls. "It was originally kind of an architectural simulation inspired by the work of a number of architectural theorists. While working on it they realized they needed to have some kind of people living in these structures until it started turning into an accumulation of little people."

Originally slated by Wright to be an architectural-development game in much of the same way that the *SimCity* series had been a city-development game, Electronic

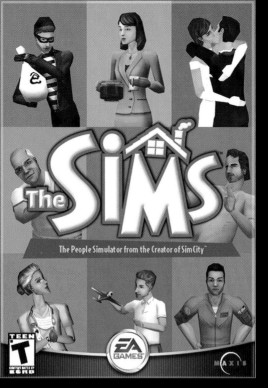

No game has quite captured the human experience and zeitgeist like the *Sims* has over the last seven years.

Arts saw a future in the project. Perhaps more of a toy than a game in the traditional sense, EA was quick to funnel resources to Wright to help grow his idea.

As Wright continued to tinker, he realized that it would be the people in the houses which would draw people to the game. Given the chance to customize a house was a draw, but the real meat of the title would be the people that inhabited the house. Originally only in the game to evaluate the houses, the actual Sims were quickly becoming the main draw. Wright continued to work on what was slowly becoming *The Sims*, and a 2000 launch date loomed.

Wright and his team could see a future for the game, and it was not just with the stand-alone title. As part of the game testing, Wright would have people come in to play the game in its current state and gauge how they played. "We would put two people in front of one computer; and they might be roommates or spouses or friends. And as they were playing the game, they were basically telling the story to each other. They were interpreting what they were seeing on the screen."

Wright and his team slowly realized that a larger community could follow based on the connection the testers felt with their Sims. Envisioning a series of stores, communities, and other player-created content on the Internet, Wright began to realize that something big was brewing.

Frank Gibeau was part of the team that helped launch *The Sims* onto the market and he remembers it well. "It was really cool for me to come in and sit down with Will Wright and some of the other guys and listen to how they were viewing the game. I mean they completely changed how it went to market."

Although excitement was building, the true question of whether people would enjoy it remained to be answered. Any and all fears about the title, however, were quickly assuaged. When February 4, 2000 hit, gamers would flock to the shelves to take in their very own Sims.

Featuring 3D sprites living in a 2D world, *The Sims* and its successors remain unique in that there is no overhead goal of the game. Simply living with and controlling Sims while playing with the environment has remained objective enough.

Similarly, the game lacked a concrete storyline for players to follow. Wright's calculations in the testing had been accurate, however. Players simply enjoyed playing *The Sims* and interpreted for themselves the interactions between players and other characters.

Every Sim has its needs, such as hunger and love, that must be met by the player. Some are

The number of games *The Sims* franchise has sold to date, making it EA's #1 best-selling franchise globally.

95 million

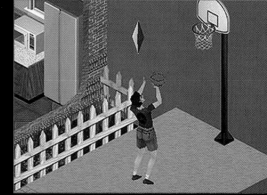

Wright sees a future with games even more interactive than *The Sims*, which is the current state-of-the-art in life simulation games.

"At its core, *The Sims* is attracting creative people, and our studio really sees itself as putting tools in the hands of creative people. And I think where we're really having a lot of fun right now is realizing how much better we can make those tools. So we don't really believe that we direct the way consumers experience *The Sims*."
—Nancy Smith

As the base game continued to fill the shelves throughout 2000, Wright and his Maxis team were hard at work on what would become the first of seven expansion packs. Featuring new characters including Santa Claus, *Livin' Large* would become standard issue for fans of *The Sims*.

Adding new features and items to the general mix of *The Sims*, *Livin' Large* quickly needed a successor that added to the gameplay as well. *House Party* would be the second of the expansion packs to hit the market, and allowed most notably for players to throw a party. Where *The Sims* prevented a house party by sending the police to a house that was getting overly rambunctious, *House Party* allowed *Sims* players to go big. With new items, music, and Sims, *House Party* truly expanded on the full *Sims* experience.

The first celebrity experience was also included in the expansion pack, as Drew Carey would hop out of his limousine to join in the revelry if the party was big enough.

The Sims was quickly establishing itself at the forefront of Electronic Arts' lineup, mostly for moving demographics. Instead of the young male audience that typically made up a game following, *The Sims* was popular with the old and young, male and female. Many casual gamers added to this mix and soon millions upon millions of the game had sold.

In 2002, after just over two years on the market, *The Sims* reached the biggest milestone in gaming. Finally taking *Myst* off its throne, *The Sims* had sold over 16 million copies of the base game, making it the top selling PC game in history. The unique open-ended gameplay, depth of the experience and easy-to-learn interface had seen *The Sims* go

the most basic: the need to eat or use the washroom, or can reflect the most complex of human emotions, such as personal growth and finding a romantic relationship.

Not understandable by any human standards, the *Sims* in the game speak Simlish, a gibberish language taking cues from many real languages that include English. Adding to the imaginative nature of the game, players were left to fill in the blanks as to what their Sims were talking about.

The Sims was instantly critically acclaimed as an innovation in the gaming world. Among its notable achievements, the base game was awarded GameSpot's PC Game of the Year award for 2000. Critics especially lauded the title for some of the original features of Wright's *Dollhouse*: the environment itself. The level of architectural detail and item selection

is an art unto itself, a fact not lost on the critics. While the *Sims* themselves took center stage, Wright's design was highly praised.

It was the players themselves, however, that ultimately had to make the decisions regarding the homes they lived in. Fully customizable from top to bottom, players could add rooms, rearrange furniture, and even burn down their houses if they weren't careful. Add pets, spouses, and children to the mix, and *The Sims* offered a plethora of ways to enjoy the game.

Perhaps the first game that actively involves watching in-game characters sleep, players also saw themselves responsible for their Sims well being in new ways. They would have to make their Sims eat, clean, exercise and even get jobs to remain happy and prosperous.

CHOOSE YOUR NIGHTLIFE.

WANT TO PLAY AGAIN?
TURN TO PAGE 40

WANT TO PLAY AGAIN?
TURN TO PAGE 40

WILL THEY BE SLAPPED AT DINNER OR DANCE
ALL NIGHT LONG? WILL THE DATE END AT
9 P.M. OR CONTINUE ON TO THE VIP ROOM?
THE NIGHT BEGINS SEPTEMBER 15TH.

The Sims 2
nightlife
EXPANSION PACK

LIVEINSIM.COM

"How would we express *The Sims*? Crayola used to be a company that only did crayons, but now you go to their section in a store and there are pens, markers, glitter and colored pencils. There's even modeling clay, paints and all kinds of paper and craft books. I think of *The Sims* that way. *The Sims* used to be only crayons, and what we're trying to do is bring as many interesting, creative tools as we can to market to really open up the inter-activity for people."

—Nancy Smith

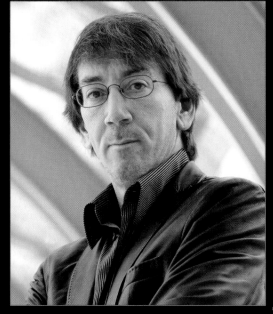

Will Wright had been working with EA for nearly the whole time the company had been in business. *The Sims* would be among his, and EA's, biggest hits.

from just another popular game to a true force.

Five more expansion packs would see a release as a follow up to the original title, but one remains the most important: Not merely adding to the stable of items in a Sim's home, *Hot Date* finally allowed Sims to travel outside of their shell and visit a mysterious Downtown.

Allowing the *Sims* to venture out of their home environments has remained an important aspect of later expansion titles and is a large part of how the series has survived and continued to thrive.

Expanding on this idea, *Vacation* would allow Sims to take their family and friends on a vacation to an exotic island. Including over 120 new items and three areas to explore, *Vacation* was one of the largest expansions to the original game. A massive growth in the neighborhood to go along with pets would be added in *Unleashed*.

One of the best supported games post-release of all time, *The Sims* was not yet done expanding: Sims began heading to a Hollywood-type land called Studio Town in *Superstar*. Much like the Downtown area of *Hot Date*, Studio Town allows Sims to become big stars. If the Sim gets popular enough, paparazzi can follow it and they can even acquire a stalker. If the talent does indeed allow a Sim to become a superstar, they can even earn the Simmy gold Statue. Sims could tap even into their inner wizard in the final expansion pack for the original title, *Makin' Magic*.

Although not the most popular title in the series, *The Sims Online* made an appearance in 2002. Despite rave reviews and the ability to interact with other human players in the game world, *The Sims Online* never seemed to resonate with players the way the original did. It does still have its fair share of players, however, and five years after its release still sees the occasional update directly from EA.

While *The Sims Online* failed to quite capture the hearts and minds that the original did, 2004's *The Sims 2* certainly grasped fans of the series and ran hard. On the immediate surface, *The Sims 2* certainly looked much better than its predecessor, with neighborhoods and houses fully rendered in 3D.

Changes to the title were more than simply cosmetic. Sims would transition through life for the first time, from being a baby all the way through old age and death (unless death had occurred while younger). Along the way, the specific needs of a Sim can change and a premium is placed on having a full family of Sims, since all will eventually die.

This unique circle of life extended beyond the grave as well. Dead Sims would periodically return to haunt the Sims still living, striking fear or even killing the ones who remained. Beyond the macabre, however, there were many more aspects of the original that were expanded upon in the sequel.

One of the biggest changes involved the neighborhoods themselves. Sims could travel right away to visit other Sims in their neighborhood, but like the first title, were limited to just that area until an expansion pack was installed. Even creating a Sim was bigger in *The Sims 2*, allowing for full customization of a Sim, including facial expressions and blinking.

As malleable as the original, *The Sims 2* enjoyed a strong online following right from the start, thanks in part to EA's Exchange which allowed an official route for players to

The Sims 2 finally allowed players to explore other neighborhoods in the game universe.

"People very often first put themselves into the game, and their family and friends, and even recreate their house. And then they're playing with a kind of strange little alternate reality game about themselves and their friends, almost like experimenting with a spreadsheet for hypotheticals."
-Will Wright

THE SIMS™
Played by

Nick Klawitter
Kitchener, ON
Canada

on the PC

Terry the pit bull terrier and his owner Tom were terrible neighbors. Terry stole bones from other dogs, chased unsuspecting cats up trees and barked at the mailman. Terry finally crossed the line when he tried one of his tricks on Porter, the dog next door. Porter was in league with the Fraternal Order of Samurai Kitties and they hatched a plan to get back at Terry. One night, Porter and the Samurai Kitties lured Terry into a dark alley where they taught Terry how dogs aren't always tougher than cats.

How do you play? thesims2.com

share their created content. As *The Sims 2* continues to grow, its community just grows right along side it.

In its effort to duplicate the success of the original, *The Sims 2* set a record by selling over one million copies in its first 10 days on the shelves. While the total is still being added to, total sales have topped out at 13 million copies. While this is still three million copies short of the original, the 13 million total is still more than any other game has ever sold– with the exception of the first *Sims*.

Just like the first game of the series, *The Sims 2* has seen a large number of expansion packs. *University* was the first, and one of the most unique *Sims* expansions to hit the shelves. Taking advantage of the growth stages of Sims, young Sims could have the opportunity to go to college towns and attend a university. Interesting features included the college band, a joining together of Sims playing instruments that allowed the collegian Sims a chance to earn some money.

Studying, socializing, and partying all play a role in the life of a collegiate Sim, making *University* perhaps the deepest of all Sims expansion packs. Sims pick their majors and graduate, thus returning them to the "real world" of the game.

Some of the expansion packs followed the lead of similar ones from the first game. *Nightlife* took aspects of *Hot Date*, including Downtown, and transformed them into areas for *The Sims 2*. *Pets* would be a spiritual successor to *Unleashed*, giving Sims more options regarding which pets to own and nurture,

along with the unique twist of giving pets a career path. *Bon Voyage* also takes much of its core from *Vacation*, with a focus on Sims travelling to other locales.

There would be other original expansion packs released for *The Sims 2*, however. One of the most recent is *Seasons*, bringing weather and seasons into the mix of the environment for the first time. *Open for Business* takes the standard working of jobs from both games and puts a small business twist on it. For the first time, player Sims can own and run a business.

After garnering awards just like *The Sims* before it, *The Sims 2* certainly moved new ground in a genre more or less created by the first game. Although not much information is yet available on the next title in the series, *The Sims 3*, it promises to give a new level of depth to *The Sims* experience.

The Sims holds an interesting legacy in the world of gaming. At the same time, it is a risk-taking first step in a genre and a best-selling blockbuster. By not following a formula from any game before it, Will Wright managed to take an idea and mold it into a concrete idea that has reached millions of gamers.

Wright's work, however, is not done. He can foresee a gaming world that can echo *The Sims*, with customization and a unique experience for everyone who plays. "Things like *The Sims*, where players can actually create stuff that other players are enjoying, means that it's not just the game company putting up this monolithic creation every so often. But more frequently what's going on in the Internet in general, is you have this very collaborative, creative set of things that players or people have built that are freely shared

amongst them kind of sideways or bottom up, rather than top down."

He can already see this vision starting in games today: "What's really interesting to me is we're starting to actually look at what the player does in a game and build player profiles to get a sense of who the player is, what they like, their skill levels, their aesthetic, what directions they would like to see the game go in, and in some sense have the game customize itself uniquely to each individual user."

As long as Wright is at the helm of the project, fans of *The Sims* can expect that their gaming world will continue to be fresh, innovative, accessible, and most of all, fun. *The Sims* has forged a new class of games and gamers, helping to take gaming from the backroom to the mainstream. ●

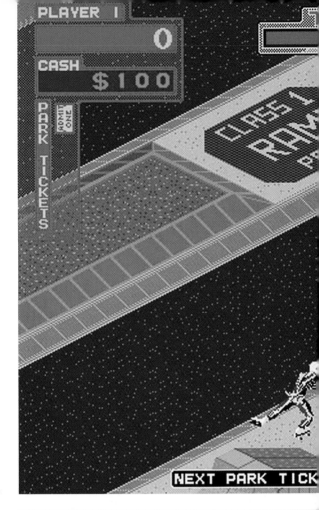

Years VI-X: Creativity
The Big Bang from Genesis to the SNES

Through its first five years, EA had become a respected leader in videogame publishing. Already a success with home gaming stateside, the company even branched into Europe in December 1986. With the start of 1987, EA was poised to break out and make its next five years twice as successful as the previous five.

EA also marked another important first in innovative that it remained sought-after with fans of the sport until the late 1990s, when it was finally replaced by newer and deeper skating games.

A popular sequel to *Seven Cities of Gold*, *Heart of Africa* was the company's first hit of the new year, racking up sales on the Commodore 64. The company had started to see the power of developing sequels to its pop-

> "What was memorable about those years at EA was everybody was very invigorated about making games. It was not very metrics driven. It was very much a question of 'Is it cool?'" —Frank Gibeau

1987: a game developed entirely in-house. Every title the company published had been made by an independent developer or a small design studio without the muscle to publish itself. Although this arrangement was working well, building an in-house development capability was another key engine for growth.

Skate or Die would become a hit on the home computer market, and perhaps more importantly, seeded the future with a whole new division of the company. The first extreme sports game, *Skate or Die* may be seen as a spiritual precursor to the games of the EA SPORTS BIG line of games. The game was so

ular games. As long as the new game could hold up with the original in terms of quality and gameplay, EA was quick to encourage its creatives to not just envision and build games, but franchises.

Also released during that time was *Chuck Yeager's Advanced Flight Trainer*. Showcasing several features of later games from EA, it served as a pioneer for some of them. Adding a realistic level of physics and flight characteristics, players could fly authentic planes including the Bell X-1 that Yeager used to first break the sound barrier. Another major innovation came in its commentary. Not only was

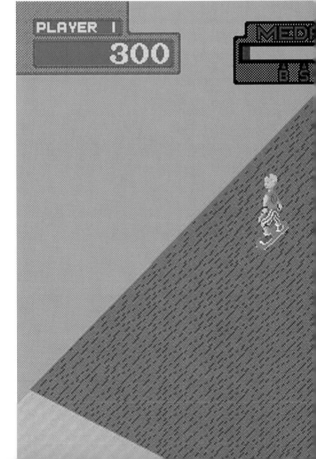

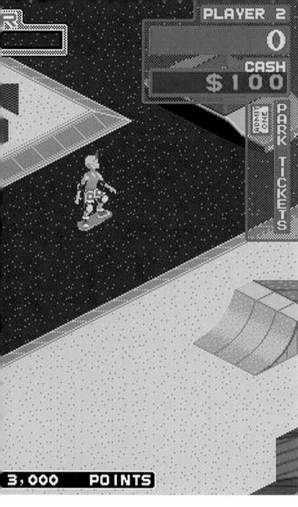

PLAYER 2
0
CASH
$100
PARK TICKETS

3,000 POINTS

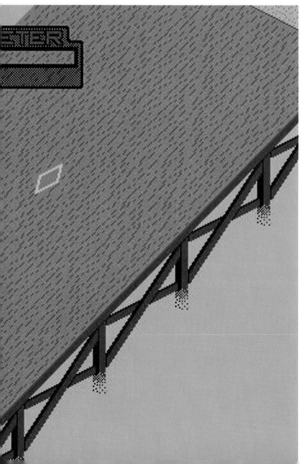

By Michael Kosaka, Stephen Landrum & David Bunch

IIGS

ELECTRONIC ARTS®

Skate or Die was the first extreme sports game and an ancestor of the EA SPORTS BIG division.

Yeager's name on the title, he lent his voice and likeness in-game, a huge innovation for the time. Yeager would even chime in sarcastically when a player crashed a plane.

Al Escudero and David Wong would debut a major RPG hit in 1987 as well: *Deathlord* set new standards for RPGs in terms of depth, difficulty, and complexity. Allowing for only one saved game at a time, and featuring 16 continents and hundreds of monsters, the game thrilled and fascinated even hardcore gamers. A second popular RPG, *Legacy of the Ancients*, also hit store shelves that year.

Earl Weaver Baseball would also break new ground for sports titles in 1987. While *World Tour Golf* was deep, and *Jordan vs. Bird* was authentic (and featured now-obligatory extras like a 3-point shootout and slam dunk contest), *Earl Weaver Baseball* was both.

Thanks to hours upon hours of strategic interviews with Weaver himself, the game displayed unparalleled artificial intelligence for the time. With Daglow's thoughtful game designing and Eddie Dombrower's contributions on the baseball end (he would even apologize to Weaver for taking up so much of his time with interviews), *Earl Weaver Baseball* was an oldschool precursor to *John Madden Football* and EA SPORTS.

Earl Weaver Baseball had several innovations in its gameplay as well. It was the first game to allow a player to play a full season with one team while allowing the computer to simulate the rest of the games, an assumed feature of today's sports games and one that

In its first year as a public company,
EA would see revenues increase to:

$100 million

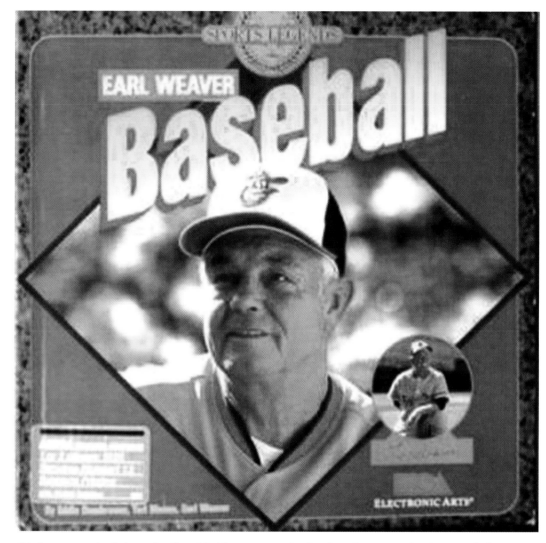

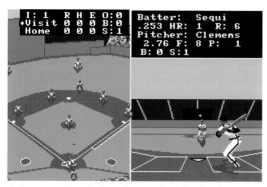

Earl Weaver Baseball set the standard for detail in a sports game and its roster update diskettes foreshadowed EA's annual sports game installments.

Earl Weaver Baseball was the precursor to the entire EA SPORTS lineup and was the first videogame to include deep player stats and teams.

didn't even make it into the first *Madden*.

Allowing for a single-game arcade mode and a manager mode, the game included different stadiums of the day and several historic fields as well. It featured a public address voice and managers who would argue calls with umpires. *Earl Weaver Baseball* also included a landmark feature for EA's later sports titles: full rosters of big league teams with real names and statistics. The game would be updated yearly with player diskettes, fore-

shadowing the annual releases of the sports titles that we see today.

1988 marked another important year in EA's history. Since the 1983 videogame crash, the company had shied away from publishing console-based games, and instead focused mainly on the personal computer market. Although Nintendo had come to dominate the home-console market by 1988, their restrictive measures on third-party developers kept EA away.

"Yeah, I was just all over the Sega Genesis launch like a cheap suit, and that's when I led the company into this much more risky and complex strategy, where I'm looking at it going, 'You know, I don't want to have one of these overlords telling us what we can and cannot do, and controlling every aspect of the business and making us constantly ask permission to blow our nose.'

So basically, I pushed the company to reverse-engineer the Sega Genesis and we had these brilliant young hackers who were able to do it. These guys were heroes. I mean, I tear up every time I think about it and think 'Wow, what a difference that made for the history of EA.'"
—Trip Hawkins

With the launch of a new system from Sega, the 16-bit Genesis (which was twice as powerful as Nintendo's system) EA saw their chance to break into the home console market. After reverse-engineering a Sega Genesis motherboard to get a jumpstart on developing games for the system, EA released several popular titles in 1988 including a racing simulator named *Grand Prix Circuit* and a small RPG called *Mars Saga*.

Developed by a startup studio named Westwood, *Mars Saga* had players take on the role of a marooned space traveler caught up in a story of drama and intrigue on Mars. The original version had to be rushed to meet its 1988 ship date, and thus the game was sent to market incomplete, including six completely useless player classes. Although *Mars Saga* offered a fresh story and showed strong potential, its unfinished feeling left gamers wanting more, and a polished version did not hit store shelves until the following year.

Despite the misstep, the small studio would remain independent for ten more years and would develop several more titles published by EA, including the blockbuster *Command & Conquer* series, leaving most to forgive and forget the rocky start.

1988 was also pivotal for EA's sports games. The first hockey title from EA, *Powerplay Hockey*, was released for the Commodore 64. It would foreshadow the appeal and success of the company's hockey games in the 1990s (such as the legendary *NHLPA '93*, which is a direct successor to the 1988 game.)

Jordan vs. Bird also broke new ground for EA in 1988. An update of the original title, *Dr. J. vs. Larry Bird*, the sequel featured a young superstar named Michael Jordan as Larry Bird's nemesis. With the increased depth of the slam dunk contest and 3-point shootout, its success would demonstrate the viability of a basketball franchise, the appeal of including mini-games, and the use of marquee players as the main marketing tool.

By 1989, EA stepped to the forefront of the home console world. Nintendo licensed the rights to 15 popular EA titles for publishing on their NES. Additionally, EA brought the first game that it developed internally to market, *Skate or Die 2*.

Developer Will Wright made a breakthrough of his own in 1989. After utilizing a level editor in developing his title *Raid On Bungling Bay*, Wright quickly discovered that he enjoyed playing with his editor more than playing the actual game. Building on this concept, he streamlined his level editor into an innovative title called *SimCity*.

A game that would one day spawn a division of its own at EA, the original *SimCity* was a game which featured no final win-or-lose objective, a rarity in most games even today. Building and managing a city may have sounded like an odd concept to some gamers at the time, but the title quickly gained a cult following and became a critical and commercial success. For those who had to have a goal in the game, several scenario modes were added. Earning award after award, *SimCity* could be found on nearly every platform of personal computer in the early 1990s.

Despite the success of *SimCity*, Peter Molyneux would not be stopped in his development of his own "God game" in 1989. His title, *Populous*, allowed players to play the role of a deity to a civilization. After molding the

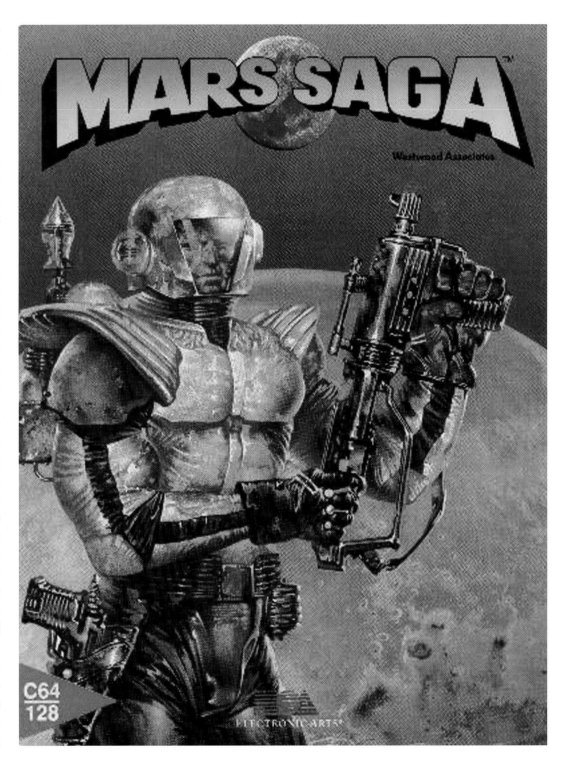

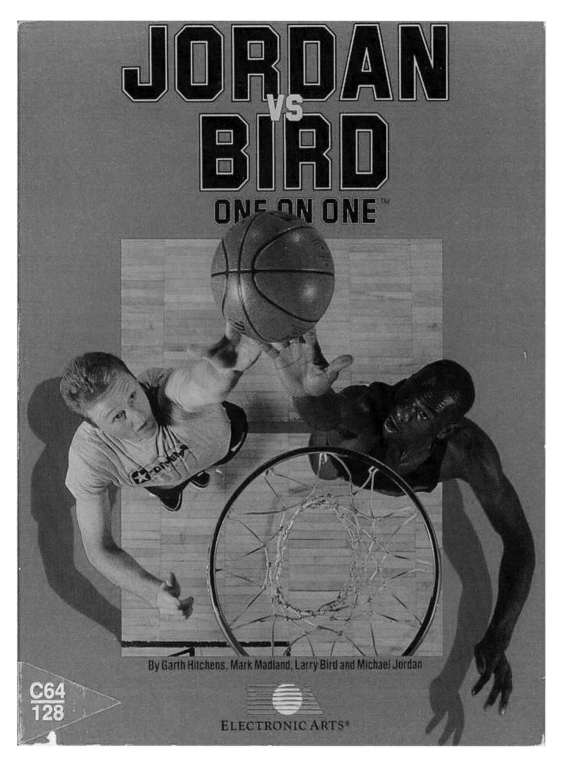

By Garth Hitchens, Mark Madland, Larry Bird and Michael Jordan

C64
128

ELECTRONIC ARTS®

community to his or her desire, the objective of the game was to then conquer a neighboring community led by an AI deity. The game would go on to spawn two innovative sequels of their own.

While the company continued to innovate and develop fresh titles, 1989 and 1990 also witnessed the incarnation of EA's greatest single franchise: *John Madden Football*. An instant hit at the time, and more popular than ever in the late 2000s, *John Madden Football* almost never made it to kickoff. Originally looked into at the behest of the heads of EA, the project was viewed as not feasible from the start. Even Madden himself had doubts, insisting that any game with his likeness on it be a realistic football simulation, with authentic rules, plays, 11-on-11 players, and timing. With the technology of the mid-80s, many observers viewed this as simply not possible.

Thanks to the hard work of EA's new internal game development team, a game was ready by late 1989. While not featuring any NFL players or teams due to licensing restrictions, and limiting players to only single games, the game instead delivered on fun, fast gameplay and made a few technological breakthroughs. Madden himself offered commentary on individual plays, an unheard-of feature at the time. And by allowing gamers to edit the extensive playbook and play the sport in a realistic simulation for the first time, the game was an instant hit and had EA pondering a sequel—a dream which would take two more years to materialize.

First released for the Apple II, *Madden* was released for numerous platforms and sold especially well on the fledgling Genesis and was a favorite of football fans everywhere.

Jordan vs. Bird showcased Michael Jordan, who was already on his way to becoming the greatest basketball player of all time.

SimCity was an unlikely hit and would spawn three sequels and scores of spinoffs.

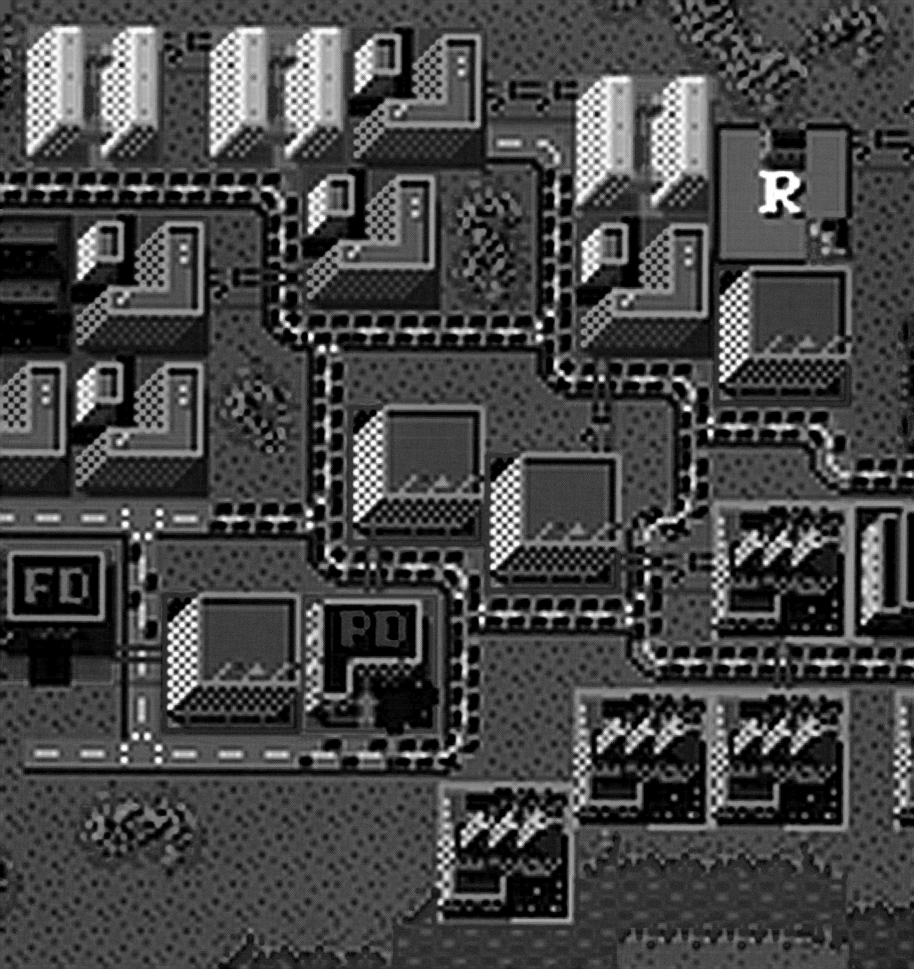

"When we were a really small company, as soon as we were done with the Friday meeting and done throwing Nerf balls, people were firing up their Genesis and playing *Madden Football*. So there was this thing happening where you could see that it was not just gaming, but it was social competition, and we said, 'Wow, this is different'."
—Chip Lange

Chip Lange, who has been with EA since 1991, fondly remembers the days of the original *Madden*. "When we were a real small company, as soon as we were done with the Friday party and done throwing Nerf balls, people were firing up their Genesis and playing *Madden Football*."

EA supported the Genesis from the get-go. In 1990, the company made its biggest bet on any console yet and delivered no fewer than nine titles for the system, the most from any third-party company at the time. The subsequent success of the Genesis would be vital in driving the success of EA. Frank Gibeau, a 16-year veteran and current head of the EA Games label, said of the early Genesis offerings, "I think we did a good job understanding how to make great games,

and reaching the customers who appreciate that. This would prove to be an important lesson over the next 15 years."

Gibeau even realized it was the passion for quality and authenticity that had attracted him to the company in the first place. "My impressions of EA were that they were a very cool company that made the best games on the market and were kind of uncompromising in their creative selections, in terms of concept and gameplay. They had the best producers and the best game makers. I kind of fell into this job...kind of randomly actually, but I was playing the games. I was the consumer as a user, and I thought they were awesome."

Two important sports titles were released in 1990. *PGA Tour Golf* was the second major golf title for the company, featuring real golf stars

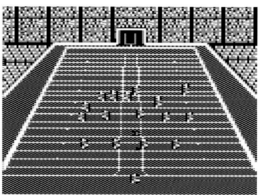

John Madden Football was seen as a one-off title; few predicted that it would become the most successful videogame franchise of all time.

and famous courses from around the world. The game would not only be a success on the Genesis, it would ship as standard software on IBM's PS/2 computer platform, with over 250,000 home machines.

The Genesis would also host its first basketball hit in 1990: *Lakers vs. Celtics and the NBA Playoffs* would capitalize on the popularity of the two dominant NBA teams of the 1980s. *Lakers vs. Celtics* would be the first 5-on-5 basketball game, in the same vein as *Madden Football*. Like its football counterpart, *Lakers vs. Celtics* was a hit and paved the way for a popular annual series, *NBA Live*.

At this stage EA was still a relatively small company and CEO Trip Hawkins would turn day-to-day control of the company over to new President Larry Probst, while leaving to form his own videogame console company, 3DO.

Current CEO John Riccitiello is quick to offer praise for his predecessor. "Larry Probst is actually one of the main reasons I originally came to EA. I don't think I've ever met anybody with a deeper reservoir of integrity about how to run a company and how to put the company first than Larry Probst."

Additionally, the company reduced its dependence on computer titles. The total revenue generated from computer games was reduced from 93 percent to 66 percent, a much healthier balance since penetrating the console market. With a new year looming, business booming, and the 16-bit console market zooming, EA's early support of the Genesis turned out to be a masterstroke. Propelled by this strength and flush with cash, the company would release several notable titles in 1991.

An old series was revived with *Bard's Tale Construction Set*. For the first time, the *Construction Set* would use an older game engine as the foundation for its builder. Based on the original *Bard's Tale* of 1985, the *Construction Set* allowed gamers to create their own adventures in the *Bard's Tale* style. They could then share the games with friends and freely distribute their own creations.

Additionally, 1991 marked the release of the first *John Madden Football* sequel, *Madden '92*. Although the new Super Nintendo had to settle for a port of the original for the time being, other 16-bit systems would get the updated, and in many ways completely new, game.

Featuring a co-op mode, single-game, season and sudden-death modes, players had the largest selection of game modes ever seen in a

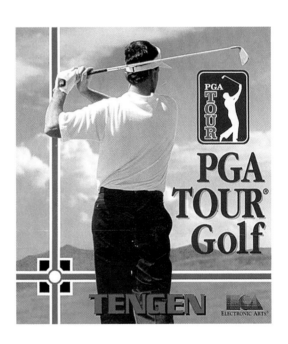

The number of home computers that
PGA Tour Golf was shipped to in 1990:

250,000

Madden '92

Although no teams were specifically featured, every NFL city and that team's colors were represented.

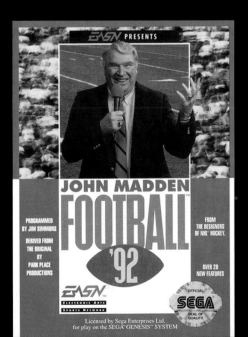

football game. Variable weather, instant replay and commentary from Madden himself would add to the experience. A popular, annoying, and now cult-favorite aspect of the game was the result of in-game injuries. *Madden '92* was notorious for its player injuries, which featured an ambulance speeding onto the field to provide medical assistance to the downed player. Unfortunately for the other players on the field, the ambulance had no concerns about them and commonly plowed through players from both teams.

Although no NFL teams or logos were specifically featured, every NFL city and that team's colors were represented in *Madden '92*. Also, the EA SPORTS Network its debut. Conceived as a fictional television network broadcasting the games on the system being played on, it offered a fresh take on game presentation. Eventually, pressure from sports television channel ESPN forced EA to drop the EASN moniker in a move that would prove to be momentous for both companies, and would eventually lead to a productive relationship between two of the most influential companies in sports today.

Marking its 10th year in business, EA's revenues increased 55-percent in 1991. The company also noted that it had generated $500 million in revenue over its first 10 years–impressive for a company that was given little chance for success in 1982.

EA punched gamers in their faces with a fresh take on racing in 1991: *Road Rash* was not only a motorcycle game that featured the fastest on-screen racing of the day, it was the first game which allowed combat between racers. While winning the race was important, knocking opponents off of their motorcycles

The original *Road Rash* was a fresh, out-of-the-box racing game that was attractive to a new generation of gamers.

(left) John Madden was a success long before his video-game. The Hall of Fame coach is seen here being carried off the field after victory in Super Bowl XII. (opposite) The injury screen in *Madden '92* brought on an ambulance that had little regard for players in its path.

in interesting ways was just as fun. The game was so successful that different versions and sequels were released through 1999.

Bulls vs. Lakers in the NBA Playoffs, also released in 1991, would not only serve as the sequel to the previous year's game, it also marked the first time EA updated a sports title annually.

Through 10 years, EA had gone from a fledgling company struggling to publish its first games to a gaming powerhouse. Some of the company's best loved titles either saw their release or conception during these halcyon days, a fact not lost on Gibeau. "The first *Road Rash, Desert Strike, Madden '92, NHLPA '93*; those are my formative EA games."

Looking back at EA after 10 years, a pattern becomes apparent: make great games, market them smartly, and people will buy them and become loyal to your brand. But even with its considerable success after just 10 years, the visionary leadership at EA could not have foreseen all the changes that were to come in the videogame industry that would help make EA and EA SPORTS household names. ●

#12 INJURED
BY #78

Hollywood studios have looked to videogames for two decades as important revenue generators.

EA Treks into Tinseltown

While technology improved over the years and new game systems like Intellivision, Colecovision, Nintendo Entertainment System, Sega Genesis, Sony PlayStation, Nintendo 64, PlayStation 2, Xbox and GameCube offered huge advances in graphical power, Hollywood's involvement in licensing rarely extended beyond the initial licensing agreement.

For the most part, Hollywood-licensed games were poor excuses for interactive entertainment. The majority of game companies, having spent anywhere from $1 million to over $10 million for a TV or movie license, had little money left in their coffers to invest in developing a quality product. Unfortunately, they counted on the movie poster on the box to sell the game, which it often did to the mass market, but not to core gamers.

By 2001, over two decades of horrible Hollywood-licensed games had left a bad taste in gamers' mouths, but Hollywood, which receives its licensing cash up front from game publishers, continued to look at videogames as the number-one licensing revenue generator for movies.

By 2002, Electronic Arts, the largest videogame publisher, had also learned how to target key Hollywood properties and turn them into solid games. In the span of a few years, the software giant signed huge, multi-year licensing deals for the Harry Potter books and films, the James Bond films, and *The Lord of the Rings* trilogy. The game maker approached each of these Hollywood properties differently, but received the same results—strong game sales.

The Boy Wizard

EA acquired the rights to the most famous wizard in the world in November 2000. The Harry Potter games were based on the literary works of J.K. Rowling, rather than just the films, which allowed the studio to focus on larger games without the limiting time constraints that Warner Bros. contended with for the films. Bypassing the movies also allowed the developers to devote all their attention to the gameplay, rather than worrying about motion-capture or Hollywood likenesses.

Harry Potter and the Sorcerer's Stone for PlayStation became one of the Top 10 best-selling games in 2001, even though it didn't ship until November. The end result: EA made back its hefty multiyear licensing investment for Harry Potter with the very first game. Since then, EA has expanded beyond the films to offer games like *Harry Potter Quidditch World Cup*, an original "sports"

AP/Wide World

game based on the broomstick-riding competitions from the film. The most recent games, including *Harry Potter and the Order of the Phoenix*, feature not only the likenesses of all of the Hollywood actors, but also many of their voices.

Neil Young, head of EA's Los Angeles based operation, said the benefit of having a broad set of rights is the ability to access not just what is on the screen but also something that is fundamental to the fiction as well.

"That was a luxury we didn't have initially with the *Lord of the Rings* property, but one that we have now after unifying the literary rights from the Tolkien Estate," said Young. "I think there's great value in being able to get all of the rights associated with a property because it gives you the opportunity to fully deliver on the fantasy. Being able to deliver something that is authentic to those fans and to fully explore this in our medium, we have a much bigger opportunity to be able to dig into the fiction," Young said.

Bond, James Bond

EA took a unique approach with the James Bond license. After years of releasing James Bond games several years after each new film came out, including *Tomorrow Never Dies* and *The World Is Not Enough*, EA decided to create original Bond games and ship them on a nearly annual basis. *James Bond 007: Agent Under Fire* and *James Bond 007: Nightfire* were the first two original Bond games introduced to gamers. Written from the ground up as a cinematic gaming experience, the end results were games that played like games rather than mere movie licenses. For *Nightfire*, EA did ante up the money for Pierce Brosnan's likeness, which was featured both in the

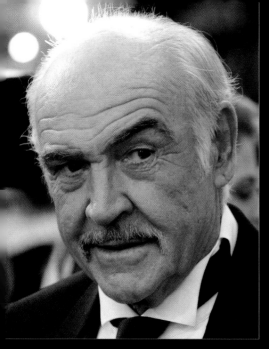

(above) Sean Connery reprised his role as James Bond for EA's take on *From Russia With Love*. (opposite) EA has made *Harry Potter* videogames that not only tie-in and extend the books' storylines, but has also published fun spin-offs like *Quidditch World Cup*.

game and on the box art. With the added exposure of MGM's feature film and 40th Anniversary DVD Collection, EA rode the game to the top of the charts.

The next original game, *James Bond 007: Everything or Nothing*, featured an all-star cast of real-life actors. The game was cast like a feature film with Pierce Brosnan in the starring role, Shannon Elizabeth assuming virtual Bond girl status as Serena St. Germaine, Oscar winner Judi Dench reprising her role as M, John Cleese as Q, Heidi Klum as bad girl Katya Nadanova, and Willem Dafoe as megalomaniac Nikolai Diavolo. Classic Bond bad guy Jaws (played by Richard Kiel) returns to action in the game, as well. The original story, which was written by James Bond movie scribe Bruce Feirstein, sends Bond after Diavolo, who has created nanotechnology that can eat through metal and bring the world's armies to a halt. Pop singer Mya not only co-wrote and sang the "Everything or Nothing" theme song, she also appears in the game as Bond girl Mya Starling.

EA focused on the villain in *GoldenEye: Rogue Agent*, the first game in the Bond franchise that doesn't star James Bond. Players assume the role of an aspiring agent who joins forces with Auric Goldfinger to battle Dr. No. Christopher Lee reprised his role as Francisco Scaramanga for this original game and Judi Dench brought the virtual M to life.

For its last James Bond game, EA turned to the MGM archives and remade the 1963 film *From Russia With Love*. The game maker even managed to lure Sean Connery out of retirement to voice Bond for the new game— although in-game Connery appears as he did in the 1963 film.

"As an artist, I see this as another way to

explore the creative process," Connery said at the time. "Videogames are an extremely popular form of entertainment today, and I am looking forward to seeing how it all fits together."

Connery was joined by other likenesses from the original cast of the film, which included Q (Desmond Llewelyn), Donald "Red" Grant (Robert Shaw), Rosa Klebb (Lotte Lenya), Tatiana Romanova (Daniela Bianchi), Kerim Bay (Pedro Armendariz) and Miss Moneypenny (Lois Maxwell). Although the publisher extended its James Bond videogame license with MGM through 2010, EA opted out of the license to focus on original properties.

The Lord of the Rings

Taking a more traditional approach, *The Lord of the Rings: The Two Towers* game combined the biggest action sequences of the first two films into one non-stop adventure experience. Utilizing the voices and likenesses of the principle characters, as well as the film's music, art, and sets, the end result was a bestseller that allowed both hardcore and casual gamers to experience the films in a unique way—by starring in the action. *The Return of the King* game was a collaborative effort that features the principal cast, as well as areas of the story that weren't explored in the film due to time constraints. Shared digital assets allowed EA's team to take digitized actors directly from the film, tessellate the models and then turn them into 3D polygonal characters that very closely resemble the actors.

We had regular video conferences with the New Zealand film production during the game production. It's rare to have direct

access to the assets, to the people who created the assets, the actors, likenesses and voices, and not just to lift that from the finished film, but to have performances specific to the game. It was important to have all of this.

"Our medium has so many things to think about: visual expression, technical expression and creative design expression," said Young. "The degree of time that you spend creating what the characters and worlds look like detracts from creating the game. We were able to focus on creating a really great game experience because we didn't have to worry about what Gandolf looked like or how the Watcher in the Water moves."

With the movies successfully completed, EA continues to create new *Lord of the Rings* games thanks to its literary rights, which brings the films and the original works together under the same game studio roof.

"The unification of the rights helped us extend the games and the game fiction," said Young. "If you think about the universe that Tolkien created, it's a vast universe that's now been imprinted indelibly by Peter Jackson's vision of what Middle Earth looks like and sounds like. We're able to explore parts of the fiction that were talked about in the books but stamp them with the visual imagery that Peter Jackson had established in the film. In *The Battle for Middle Earth II* we were able to bring fictional aspects that were only mentioned in the books and explore them in the games and expansion packs."

The Godfather

EA once again turned to classic Hollywood for its first crime story game. The game maker licensed *The Godfather* from Viacom

Consumer Products and turned to original actors Marlon Brando, James Caan and Robert Duvall to reprise their roles from the films. Brando brought Don Vito Corleone to life before the actor passed away. Caan and Duvall brought Sonny Corleone and Tom Hagen to a whole new generation of gamers as their characters are featured in the game and work directly with the player.

The videogame, which draws inspiration from both Mario Puzo's book and Francis Ford Coppola's 1972 movie, allows gamers to create their own mob character and work their way up the criminal chain from petty theft to drive-bys and extortion to control of the Corleone family in a virtual New York spanning 1945-55.

EA is currently working on a new *Godfather* game that will further blend new story lines with the original characters and fiction. The first *Godfather* game was released across all platforms.

Steven Spielberg

After creating the concept for the original *Medal of Honor WWII* game at DreamWorks Interactive—a company Spielberg sold to EA before the game shipped and turned into a blockbuster franchise—Steven Spielberg has returned to EA. He's signed a three-game deal to develop original intellectual properties with EA's Los Angeles Studio over the coming years. While all of the games are still untitled, a puzzle game for Wii was demoed for the first time in public

THE LORD OF THE RINGS

II

THE BATTLE FOR MIDDLE-EARTH

at the E3 Media Summit in Santa Monica. The second game is a next-generation action/adventure game in which the player will develop a relationship with a computer-controlled female character.

"If you think about the ultimate destination for those types of relationships, it's really a true collaboration with Steven Spielberg," said Young. "We're creating three original products with one of the greatest storytellers of all time to deliver things nobody has ever seen before. We want to create three unique distinct gaming experiences that combine his expertise with EA's."

The fact that the first game shown to the press was a puzzle game for the Wii surprised some people, but this is exactly the type of mass-market game EA and Spielberg want to make.

"I think the expectation when you partner with Steven Spielberg is that every game is going to be derivative of a movie he might have made," said Young. "That's not the intent of the collaboration. At one end of the spectrum we hope to make great story-based games that connect you and non-playable characters in an emotional way. At the other end of the spectrum we hope to provide visceral, fun experiences that revolve fun activities and characters. There might be a third point on the continuum where we start to deliver things that are a bit more progressive in the canvas that we paint the game design on."

The Convergent Future

Although EA began as a game company, Young said the ultimate goal is to become a media and entertainment company. He said the blurring of lines between traditional and interactive entertainment will open up new opportunities for the company.

"With a game like *Command & Conquer 3* we created 45 minutes of live-action narrative that players got to experience as they played the game," he said. "This type of content could be distributed via IPTV and carved up and distributed in different ways."

Young said EA wants to be a leader in entertainment, and although it all starts with games, everything will merge together over time.

Young has watched as games have gone from being at the low end of the licensing totem pole, where you had a cup, a t-shirt and a game, to now where games are at the very core of the creation of the intellectual property. Whether it's a licensing partnership or a collaborative partnership, he said it's hard to think of a transmedia property (a game that has a film associated with it or a film that has a game associated with it) that aren't really highly synchronized.

"I think we've moved up the food chain and we're now peers with the people that are making intellectual properties in other mediums like film and television. I think that as EA grows from a game company to a media and entertainment company, we'll selectively and carefully take franchises and move them to other media. Whether that's taking *The Sims* and turning it into a 20th Century Fox film or taking *Madden* and turning into a hit TV show on ESPN, this is something you'll see more of. This will allow us to enable great creative expressions within these media, increase the cultural impact of the titles we're making, or whether it's just for good business; it's an inevitable direction for an IP creator like EA," Young said.

As technology continues to expand at

(above) Steven Spielberg worked closely with EA on the *Medal of Honor* titles. (opposite) *The Godfather* game put a new spin on the classic movies and featured many of the film's actors reprising their original roles.

(above) Neil Young has ably led EA's charge into Hollywood and has helped make movie-licensed games respectable. (opposite) *Command & Conquer 3* features over 45 minutes of live-action narration, a staple of the series.

rapid pace and new videogame systems are introduced in 2008 and beyond, the line between what's feasible in videogames and what's feasible on the big screen will eventually disappear. Hollywood producers are already turning established game franchises into blockbuster movie franchises. And games are beginning to explore new routes for licensed films.

"The last two to three years we've seen a convergence of the pipelines of both Hollywood talent and visual effects in games," said Young. "Today it's relatively easy to take someone from the Hollywood visual effects industry and transfer them to the games industry."

Young has been active in Hollywood convergence from his teenage years, when he worked with former Shiny Entertainment founder Dave Perry to create a game based on The Terminator. Back in those days, there was no motion-capture studio and the cartridges couldn't even support actors' voices, let alone their likenesses. A lot has changed over the years, especially over the past five years or so.

first, the movie or the game, will become a moot point inside of three years.

"I'm excited about a future in which a table of creative minds are not defined by which medium they come from, whether it be television, movies or games, but as creators of content that can successfully bridge multiple mediums," Young says.

Collaboration between Hollywood writers, filmmakers, composers and actors is already ongoing. But what the game industry is experiencing now with the recent launches of Xbox 360, PlayStation 3 and Wii is just the beginning of convergence potential.

"Television and movies are around today because of the great creative people the industry has, and the business models they have created. Game makers need to learn from that," said Young. "The entertainment industry can learn the value of a team working collaboratively on a project and the marriage between technology and art that allows for the creation of games. I think it will be interesting to see what models game makers can learn from traditional media and vice versa." ●

Years XI-XV: Growth
EA Takes Games to the Next Level

By year 11, EA's growth curve was steeper than Moore's Law, but the company was not about to level off. "It was like trying to jump on a train that was going 500 miles an hour," reflects Nancy Smith. Videogames would go mainstream in the 1990s and EA helped drive the evolution.

Several hit titles helped the company post record earnings and deliver strong growth in the stock market in 1992, and EA would continue to define the state-of-the-art in terms of quality. A new development studio called Raven Studios would release their first title, a popular RPG called *Black Crypt*. While the title had an immersive story and strong gameplay on the Amiga platform, the customizable heroes were the true story of the game. Instead of having a pre-fabricated set of characters to control, each gamer was responsible for creating his own heroes from a group of diverse classes.

Popular metal band Mötley Crüe was featured in their own game called *Crüe Ball*. Originally designed by a team of pinball machine artists, the game also featured an original soundtrack along with the band's songs.

With the American engagement in the

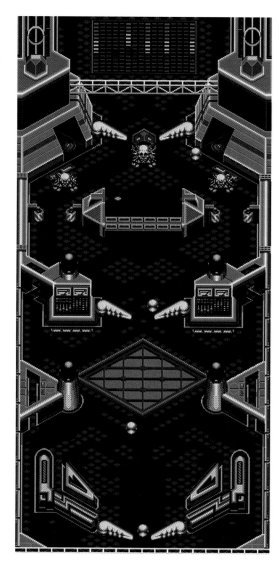

Gulf War, action-packed war games were popular in the early 1990s. EA released *Desert Strike*, a game that became the first of a five-part series. Featuring the unique concept of flying a combat helicopter from a three-quarters view, it was fun, original and relevant.

Sleuthing games were also prominent in 1992. *The Lost Files of Sherlock Holmes* was an innovative puzzle/adventure game that allowed players to interact as the popular fictional character to solve cases. A single, bigger, more complex case was featured in

"As the company grew, EA was able to move from being predominantly a North American business to Europe, and then into Japan."
—Don Mattrick

(opposite) Crüe Ball, featuring metal band Mötley Crüe, helped propel EA into mainstream entertainment.
(above) *Black Crypt* was a popluar 1992 RPG.

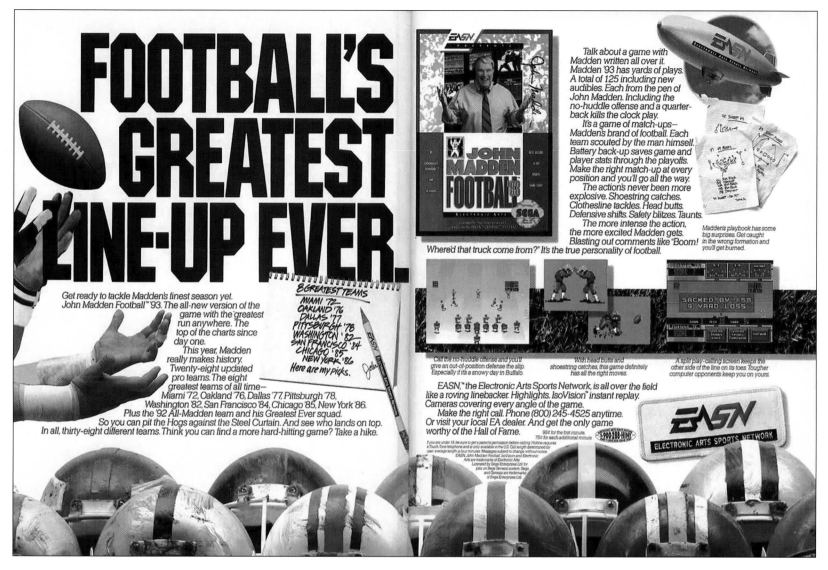

the educational-slanted title *Where in the World is Carmen Sandiego?*

EA was also active on the sports front in 1992. John Madden was back with a boom in *Madden '93*, the latest update in his young series, and the start of an annual update pattern that continues today.

For the first time, *Madden* featured historical teams, allowing gamers the chance to compete against some of football's all-time greatest players of the day. While team names were still not involved, the play-

books were deeper than ever. New additions included the ubiquitous split-screen play calling and features such as kneeldowns and ball spiking to control the clock. While the old ambulance was gone, injuries would remain in the name of authenticity.

The title broke ground in the hockey world and sold well throughout North America. With greats such as Wayne Gretzky and Jeremy Roenick in the game, the title was even featured in the 1996 movie *Swingers*. The cameo for the game

(opposite) The *Strike* series turned out to be one of the more popular franchises for EA in the the 1990s.

(above) *Madden '93* was the deepest *Madden* yet, featuring new playbooks and historical teams.

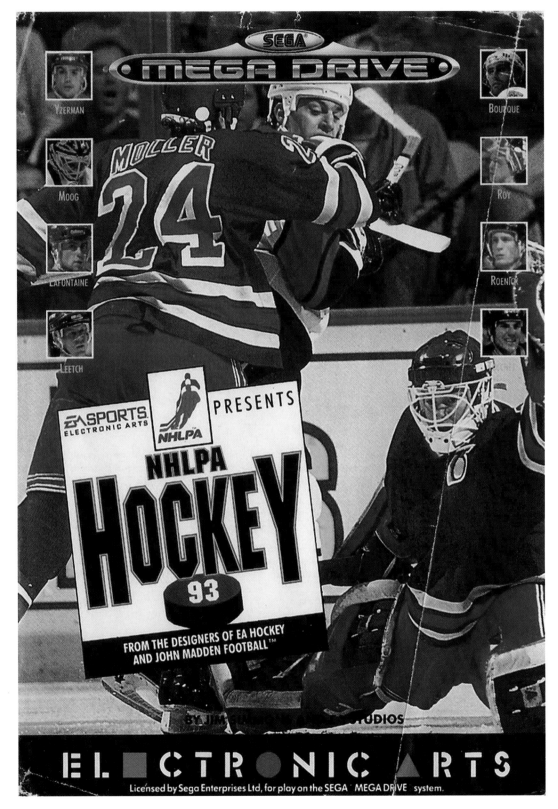

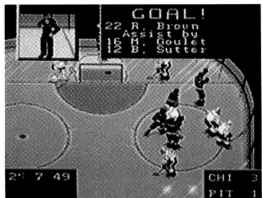

NHLPA Hockey '93 is a cult classic, still considered one of the best hockey games of all time. The game was featured proudly in the 1996 movie *Swingers*.

highlighted one of its most notable features: fighting and injuries. Without the NHLPA's license and hence its approval, EA's programmers included the ability to knock another team's players out of the game with a well-timed check. If the timing was right, two players could even drop the gloves and settle things with their fists. This "in the game" realism would anger the NHLPA but has remained a constant, if not more politically correct, goal for EA's sports offerings from the Genesis to the current day.

With the global appeal of Michael Jordan's Chicago Bulls in the early 1990s, EA released *Bulls vs. Blazers* in a continuation of their basketball series. While *NBA Live* was still a few years away, *Bulls vs. Blazers* continued to innovate and entertain. The title would offer the most comprehensive NBA lineups yet, with all 16 teams that made the playoffs represented with their complete rosters. Gamers could play one game or a full playoffs schedule, and each team's logo was present on the court.

Sharp-eyed fans would notice a new marquee on the advertising board of the game: EA SPORTS. While EASN was still in use, the first appearance of this new moniker was notable because it would soon be the name of the most successful division at EA.

Adding some international flavor, a game featuring the legendary 1992 Dream Team was also released. Setting the stage for event-specific titles seen later in the decade, *Team USA Basketball* featured the Olympic tournament in all of its glory. Unique for its time, the game also included full rosters for the international opponents.

EA's Lotus series of games debuted on platforms from the Amiga to the Genesis, offering fast-paced racing action. While popular, racing that year was more popular on two wheels. *Road Rash* was a hit in its first incarnation, and its sequel would be no different. Featuring upgradable new bikes, the game offered faster gameplay as well. With all-new tracks and a smarter AI, it became one of the most popular Genesis titles of the time.

Building off the momentum of 1992, EA sped into 1993. One of the most original titles launched that year was *Haunting Starring Polterguy* for the Genesis. Taking an amusing slant on the horror genre, the player was a ghost trying to drive a family from one of five homes. A sequel to *Desert Strike* would be released in 1993 as well. Just as popular as the first, *Jungle Strike* would take the concept to the rainforest.

One of EA's most popular titles of 1993, *SimCity 2000*, took the popular and critically-acclaimed *SimCity* and improved and updated it dramatically. Featuring increased

depth, detail, and all new natural disasters, it was an immersive experience unmatched at the time. With a three-dimensional map, the game included rivers and mountainous terrain. Underground, subways and utility pipes presented new challenges to aspiring city builders. A winner of countless awards, the game stands up even today.

The latest update of *Madden Football* included NFL team rights for the first time. After using just city names as placeholders, *Madden '94* finally allowed for the real teams and logos to be represented in the game. With a bold "EA SPORTS" script on the game box, the title sequence included a new screen: gamers would be greeted by the new logo and hear the words "EA SPORTS: It's in the Game."

Madden was not the only football game EA published in 1993. *Mutant League Football*, while built on the *Madden* engine, provided an interesting twist on the traditional game. With fire pits, lava, landmines and other hazards dotting the landscape, *Mutant League Football* featured teams of mutated misfits bent on (sometimes literally) crushing their opponents.

Hockey fans were not left in the cold in 1993. *NHL '94* added new clubs to the mix and included the license to use full teams. With the gameplay fine-tuned to be more realistic, the game now enabled fans to play an entire season, including playoffs. The fighting and blood were removed from the game, but *NHL '94* still enjoys the distinction of being mentioned as not just one of the best sports games of all-time, but one of the best games, period.

While NBA fans were waiting for their

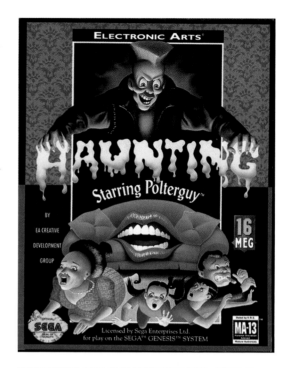

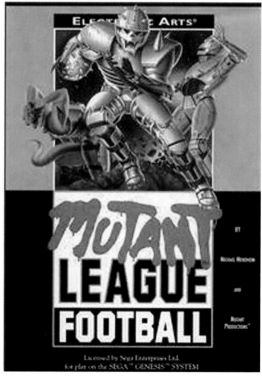

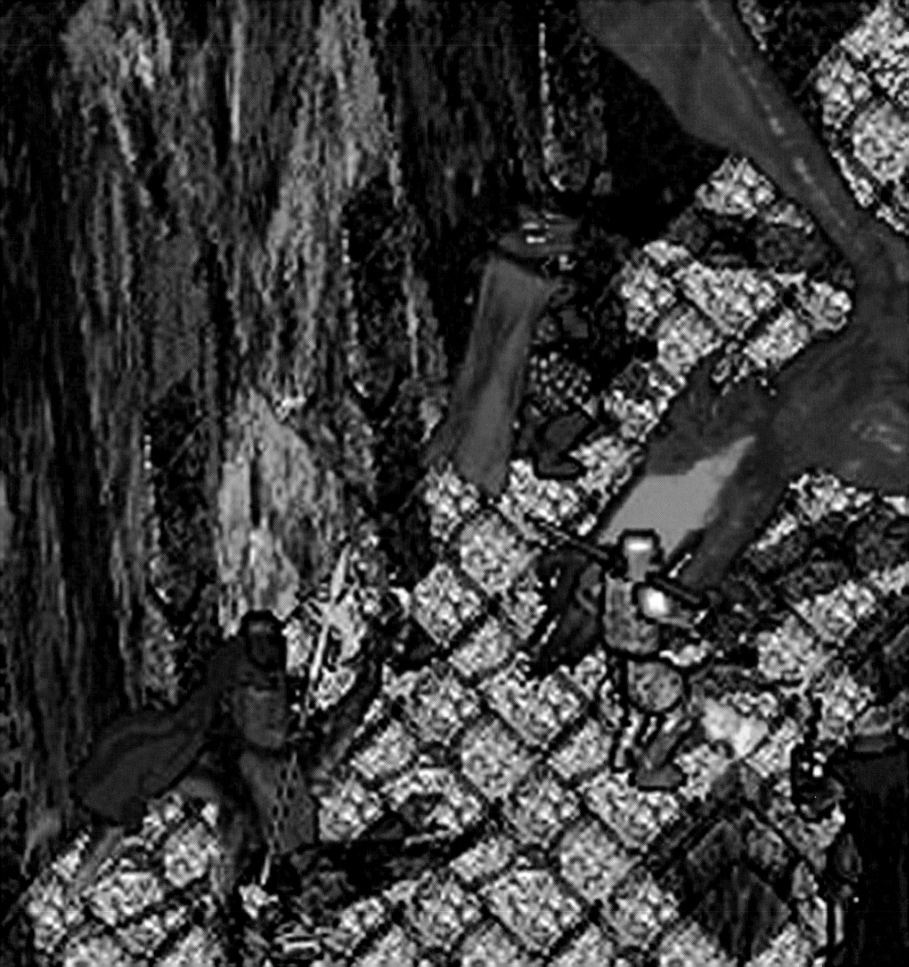

Ultima Online

One of EA's most popular
its way onto computers

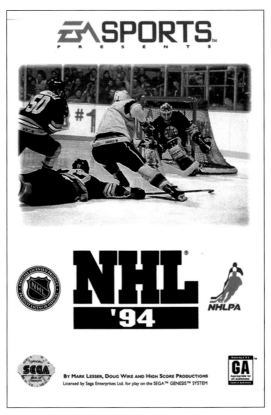

own league-dedicated franchise in 1993, they still had a game to assuage their basketball jones with *NBA Showdown*.

As 1994 approached, the ball was bouncing EA's way. The World Cup was coming to the United States for the first time and soccer was enjoying its biggest boom in North America in more than two decades. With a unique opportunity to capitalize on the game's renewed popularity, EA SPORTS seized the moment and delivered a title that would become a yearly worldwide bestseller and help give the company a global presence.

FIFA International was the first title in

titles of 1993 would find the world over.

what has become a hugely successful series for EA. Presented from a dynamic diagonal point of view, the game featured only international squads. The Sega CD version even featured video introductions and was an extremely polished product for the time. While *FIFA* was originally intended to be a one-shot game, EA picked up the series two years later and it was on its way to worldwide fame.

With the 16-bit market reaching its peak in 1994, EA delivered its tenth straight year of profitability and looked ahead to the 32-bit consoles, which were already available in Japan. Applying the lessons it learned from getting a jumpstart on the Genesis, EA embraced the Sega Saturn and Sony PlayStation.

While the two systems were still a year away from North American release, EA rolled out some of its most popular titles for the Japanese versions including *Madden, PGA Tour Golf*, and *Road Rash*. *Wing Commander III*, EA's first "interactive movie" also proved to be a hit and would sell well enough to span several continents and consoles.

With business booming in the 16-bit arena and the company making its first foray into the new technology overseas, Trip Hawkins was in the process of bringing 32-bit gaming to American consumers with his own system. After leaving EA, the ever-entrepreneurial Hawkins staked himself in a new venture called 3DO. A a system which operated on CDs. The console was expensive and didn't sell well, but it did serve as a showcase for EA's latest games.

Allowing for full-motion video to be displayed for the first time in the U.S. on a videogame system, nearly every game got a video-intro sequence. With a chance to hone their skills on the 3DO and in Japan, EA's game developers would be more than ready to tackle the 32-bit platforms when they came stateside in 1995.

The *Strike* series of games made its final 2D appearance on the Genesis and Super Nintendo in 1994. *Urban Strike* was a worthy sequel, ensuring that the series would live on in the 32-bit systems. For the first time in the series, the game included third-person elements with the main character playing on foot for portions of the story.

RPGs were also well represented in 1994 with the continuation of 1993's *Ultima VII*. *Ultima VII: Serpent's Isle* was not just a continuation of the previous year's title, it was an entirely new game within the story of the earlier title. Released for both Windows and the Super Nintendo, it provided a conclusion to one of the most popular games in perhaps the biggest RPG of all time.

With the success of *FIFA* at the start of the year, EA SPORTS extended a new franchise to fans of the NBA as well. Finally including all NBA teams and players (excluding Michael Jordan and Charles Barkley), *NBA Live '95* raised the bar for hoops games on any platform.

Madden fans also got an update in 1994. While not as innovative as some of its predecessors, it still included several new features. For the first time, the game included player names and not just jersey numbers.

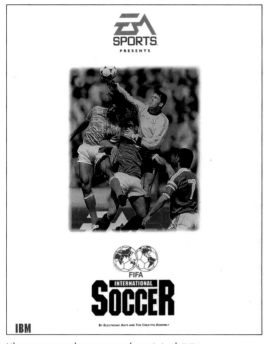

Like so many other games, the original *FIFA International Soccer* was intended to be a one-shot game. The franchise has turned out to be a valuable catalyst for EA's international operations.

In *NHL '95*, realistic features like drop passes and shot blocking were included in the game for the first time, and rosters were expanded to include more players per team. Although plagued by some software bugs, the game was still a success.

With 1994 coming to a close, 1995 would usher in the dawn of a new gaming era. Cartridges had ruled the home console arena for over a decade, but now a new storage medium that was cheaper and held a lot more data was coming to the forefront: CD-ROMs allowed games to be bigger, better looking, feature real music cuts, and include full-motion video sequences.

Fiscally, 1995 would be a soft year for EA. While the company would still turn a large profits and make shareholders happy, the 16-bit era was winding down and the installed base of early adopters who bought the 32-bit systems was just too small.

Despite the transition in the console market, other platforms thrived. Computer games and overseas markets were growing at a fast rate. In fact, EA would nearly double 1994's computer game revenues.

Flight simulator fans were thrilled by one of the best PC fighter jet games to date, *Advanced Tactical Fighters*. Putting gamers in the cockpit of some of the world's most advanced aircraft, the game provided a deep simulation of flying, as well as combat.

While games were still being developed for the 16-bit market, the 32-bit market was starting to take off. In the United States, it would be Sony's PlayStation taking the early lead in popularity, followed closely by Sega's Saturn. Larry Probst looks back and notes that even with an aggres-

sive and well-planned business strategy, Lady Luck still wielded a fateful hand. "That's another significant time in our history when we decided to very aggressively support Sony. We were able to negotiate an extremely favorable economic relationship with Sony on the PlayStation. Lucky for us, or fortuitous for us, Sony became the leading platform provider, and EA was best positioned."

Electronic Arts would release 13 titles for the PlayStation in the year, with several scoring big. *Crusader: No Remorse* was an early hit that featured full-motion video sequences and got rave reviews for its depth, including the ability to destroy just about everything in the player's environment.

Advanced Tactical Fighter was among the most detailed flight simulators of its time.

"To bring EA SPORTS to Europe was always a challenge, but it wasn't until we created the *FIFA* franchise that we had one pillar."
—David Gardner on how EA built its international presence

1995

Electronic Arts would release 13 titles for the PlayStation in the year, with several scoring big including *Road Rash, NBA Live* and *FIFA Soccer*

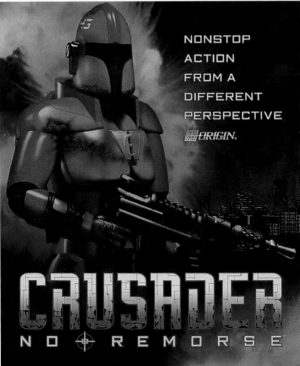

NONSTOP
ACTION
FROM A
DIFFERENT
PERSPECTIVE
ORIGIN.

CRUSADER
NO REMORSE™

Crusader: No Remorse allowed gamers to destroy nearly everything in their path. (opposite) Sony's PlayStation helped to bring EA games to a broader audience than ever before.

Road Rash, *NBA Live* and *FIFA Soccer* all sold well, while the brand new *Need for Speed* game showcased the stunning graphical capabilities of the new machine's processor. Don Mattrick, President of EA Worldwide Studios, was immediately drawn to the exotic cars of the new racing franchise, commenting that "they gave me a great excuse to have a whole stable of them and spend time thinking about what great car simulators are like."

EA's top-selling sports franchise that year was not perennial favorite *Madden* or even *NBA Live*. Instead, *FIFA '96*, produced by a new publishing house in Germany, took the top spot and helped position EA as a competitor for market share on a worldwide stage.

Remaining selective in its 16-bit offerings was a priority for EA in the transitional year, but that didn't stop a new sports title from becoming a bestseller. Building on the success and features of *Earl Weaver Baseball*, EA utilized the same formula to appeal to fans of the national pastime with *EA Triple Play Baseball '96*.

Although not a worldwide bestseller in 1995, *Madden* was still innovative and popular. In the '96 installment, gamers could create a player for the first time, which means they could recreate themselves or just about anyone they wanted to play in the game. The 3DO version also included *Madden's* first use of in-game video, most notably the cheering video that would play after a field goal or extra point. While not released in 1995 for the Saturn or PlayStation, *Madden* looked great on the 3DO and the game showcased the speed and fluidity of the next-generation consoles.

Using EA SPORTS' new Virtual Stadium technology, NHL '96 allowed gamers to view the action from multiple angles for the first time. The game would break ground graphically as well, featuring a new 3D environment on which the 2D players skated.

With the installed base of PlayStations and Saturns growing in 1996, EA was ready to pounce with new games and cool updates to existing franchises.

Ultima was updated in 1996 with the publication of *Ultima VIII*. While the game was successful, a version that teased a connection to the Internet generated the most buzz.

Featuring more tongue-in-cheek humor and violence than its predecessor, *Crusader: No Regret* capitalized on its prequel's success and became one of the top PlayStation titles of the year. Fans of the *Strike* series also got a next-gen sequel with the release of the *3D Soviet Strike*.

The company also brought two wildly successful PC games to the PlayStation. Both *Diablo* and *Command & Conquer: Red Alert* saw incredible success not only in their target audiences, but also among casual gamers for their innovative features and simple interfaces. *Diablo* featured a map that changed randomly every time a new game was started, resulting in a unique game experience every time. In *Red Alert*, the Allied vs. Soviet theme would finally be played out on a home console. Both ports were well-received and maintain popular followings to the present day.

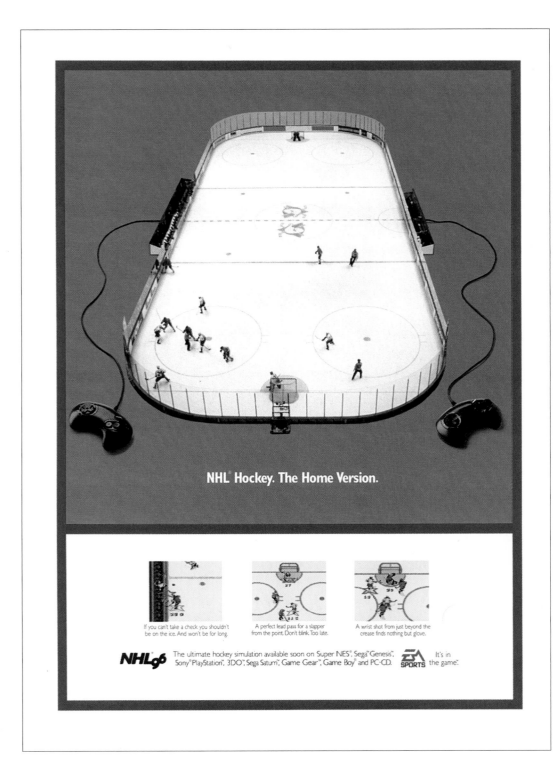

NHL® Hockey. The Home Version.

If you can't take a check you shouldn't be on the ice. And won't be for long.

A perfect lead pass for a slapper from the point. Don't blink. Too late.

A wrist shot from just beyond the crease finds nothing but glove.

NHL 96 The ultimate hockey simulation available soon on Super NES®, Sega® Genesis®, Sony® PlayStation®, 3DO®, Sega Saturn®, Game Gear®, Game Boy® and PC-CD. **EA SPORTS** It's in the game.

With a year of experience in working with the new platforms, the EA SPORTS design and publishing teams were able to take their productions to new heights.

Madden received an intense graphical update, if not an entirely new game engine. Featuring a better frame rate and faster load times, it sold well on multiple platforms. *Madden '97* for the Genesis was the last of the 16-bit Madden games.

Hockey fans got the newest game engine in 1996. Taking advantage of the muscular graphics processors in the new systems, *NHL '97* looked better than any previous game in the series. Building on the 3D arenas from *NHL '96*, the game shifted to a fully 3D look—players included. Improved graphics were evident in the goaltenders' gear—each had their personal mask and art, a concept highlighted in the game's "Mask Viewer." The game engine worked so smoothly that it would remain essentially unchanged for the next five years.

While *Triple Play Baseball* and *NBA Live* were updated, the *FIFA* soccer franchise would again prove to be the biggest hit. An unprecedented number of teams would take part in *FIFA '97*, the first time international club teams would be represented by the series. The game also featured new motion captured animations and a popular 6-on-6 indoor soccer mode.

The start of EA's second decade was marked by spectacular growth and new technology. While weathering the transition to 32-bit platforms, EA's third five-year period was marked not only by development successes, but commercial successes as well. Revenues grew and the stock

SCIENTIFIC PROOF THAT BLOOD CAN BOIL IN BELOW FREEZING TEMPERATURES.

No other game is as fast. As furious. Or as hard-hitting. It's so relentless, your heart will stop long before the action does. **NHL HOCKEY 96** The Video Game

NO MATTER HOW MUCH SOAP YOU USE YOU'LL NEVER GET IT OUT OF YOUR BLOOD.

This is it. Football's ultimate judge. The biggest. Baddest. Toughest game ever. Down and dirty. The way John likes it. **MADDEN NFL 96** The Video Game

prices climbed as Larry Probst and the new corporate leadership ably demonstrated the acumen to drive the company upward and onward.

Thanks to the addition of European studios and wider game distribution, EA was becoming nearly as well-known overseas as it was in the U.S. Even Japanese gamers, famous for shunning American software, could appreciate the exceptional advances in EA's games on their Sega Saturn and Sony PlayStation hardware.

Despite the rising popularity of the EA brand, cultural barriers still existed in overseas markets. "I think our challenge very initially was that we were the ugly Americans. We came in with big ideas about how we were going to change the market and go direct and do all this stuff and people didn't want the status quo changed and they certainly didn't want damn foreigners doing it. So our challenge at that point was to really earn respect and then to do the right thing for the company and the industry, which we did," recalls Executive Vice President David Gardner.

EA developed a strategy and stuck to it. "Our first plan was to take our existing catalogs—and the products at that time had all been done in the U.S.—and bring them to the European consumers. To do that, we had to tap into the development community in Europe," comments Gardner.

With a broader vision in place for the mid-90s, EA was ready to take its business and games to new heights in the later part of the

decade. While the massive success of the PlayStation was a key contributor to EA's continued success, the quality of its games was still the key. With steady cash flow and the technology still relatively fresh, EA was primed to shine on a 32-bit stage that was fast becoming a global market. ●

By the mid-1990s, EA was building a worldwide presence by customizing and marketing multiple sports titles across the globe.

Fall Out Boy

EA Trax Tunes in the Music Industry

Electronic Arts has been instrumental in changing the way videogames utilize music. From the early days of gaming, back when beeps and blips dominated the landscape, music was mostly an afterthought by game publishers. Instead, developers tried to squeeze as much graphics out of the console memory as possible. Later, as CD-ROM based consoles like PlayStation, Dreamcast and later DVD-ROM consoles like PlayStation 2, Xbox and Xbox 360 entered the marketplace, game makers had more room to focus on music. But the industry took the easy way to music by licensing music from established bands and including them as background music in games.

That all changed with the launch of EA Trax in 2001. EA lured long-time music executive Steve Schnur to its game studio and named him worldwide executive of music and marketing for EA. Schnur began his career at MTV, where he was part of the original programming team during the network's formative years. Prior to joining EA in 2001, he held various executive positions with the Warner Music Group, EMI and BMG, and has supervised and produced music for films including *Cruel Intentions* and

Miss Congeniality.

Schnur is responsible for the pursuit, creation and continuous development of the global vision for music in EA games. In only five years, Schnur's unprecedented innovations in bringing together the worlds of music and gaming led The Washington Post to call him "The Clive Davis of the videogame industry." He has brought established stars, breakthrough new artists and award-winning composers to such top-selling EA franchises, with *Madden NFL* as the premiere game franchise to launch a new band or introduce a new song.

"The evolution was created for us whether we liked it or not because record labels depended for decades on radio," said Schnur. "They got a break in the 80s with MTV, which gave music companies new and exciting ways to expose artists to massive amounts of people. But then MTV and radio began to go sour on them for all the understandable reasons. MTV found it makes more money creating programming than playing videos. Radio became consolidated. I like to remind people that just because these events occurred doesn't mean young people (10 to 25) still didn't crave new music. They didn't

AP/Wide World

Ozzy Osbourne

have a place where they could find it. They could be dictated the Top 25 according to radio stations. They couldn't find the level of music that we had access to. Ironically, when the discovery of music failed people, most of those people were playing videogames."

With Schnur at the helm, EA has accelerated the importance of music in games. He convinced record studios to gravitate to the most important real estate of the new century and bring music to where kids were, rather than force them to where they weren't.

"The evolution, if you look back from radio, cassette tapes to MTV to pirate video when consolidation took over, the Internet, file sharing, and now to games, is quite natural," said Schnur. "We take our real estate and rather than musically preach what people had been hearing for the last 10 or 15 years, we gave gamers a real reliable place that they knew they could come to no matter what title they played. They know they discovered *Franz Ferdinand* in *Madden* two years ago and I loved them and I wonder who I'm going to discover going forward. We've yet to let people down on that. There's always pressure, but we stand our ground that we're going to take risks musically-speaking and we're going to always make sure gamers know that if they buy a *Sims* game, *Madden* game or *Need for Speed* game, they can expect to hear something exciting musically."

Schnur has changed the music industry's perception of videogames from simple licensing opportunities to their now-essential role in artists' careers. His EA Trax initiative resulted in the first RIAA certified

Platinum videogame soundtrack with *NBA Live 2003*, and established the collaborative partnership with legendary hip-hop lifestyle company Def Jam to produce the landmark *DEF JAM Vendetta*, as well as *Def Jam: Fight for New York* and *Def Jam Icon*. In 2004, Schnur spearheaded the creation of Next Level Music, EA's groundbreaking joint venture with Cherry Lane Publishing. In 2005, he created EA Recordings and Artwerk, a digital record label focused on the distribution of EA's enormous collection of scores and songs.

"At the end of the day, each franchise has to have it's own musical personality," said Schnur. "You can't play to everyone. If you have 25 songs in *NBA Live*, you can't just have one song from each genre. You have to create personalities just like radio stations used to do. It needs to be a place to discover new music and also play homage to the property that's being discovered with it. It has to make sense. Sports games are different than lifestyle games. With *NBA Live* we took a stance five years ago that hip hop would rule. This was a time when people were still a bit uncomfortable with hip hop in the mainstream. Hip hop is now one of the most mainstream musical genres there is."

When it comes to the perennial champion, *Madden*, which has sold over 60 million units and generated over $2 billion since launch, Schnur said whether it's rock music or hip hop, the harder the better. "Gamers are about to get on the virtual field and pound some flesh and the music really needs to pump them up," he said.

"Lifestyle games like *Burnout* or *Need for*

Speed need to service a purpose emotionally and fill the environment and make it realistic," said Schnur. "The thing that's the hardest is to not follow the rules of the marketplace, but to lead. Hip hop is the most pop musical genre there is. We know that most people who are musically interested want to know what's next. You can't just put hip hop in *Burnout* because it's popular. You have to be true to what the game is. You have to be true to what we feel people want to discover. We think rock is getting more aggressive. There's an underground rock movement right now that we think is astonishingly good. We feel we have to chase that rather than chase the popular mainstream. If you don't hear a song from *Burnout* on the radio for two years, that's okay, at least you know where you heard it first."

Schnur has been profiled by the *New York Times*, *London Financial Times*, and *CNN*. He was selected as "One Of The Most Creative People In Entertainment" by *Entertainment Weekly*, both "One of the Most Powerful People in the Music Business" and "One of the Top 20 Power Players in Digital Entertainment" by *Billboard Magazine*, and "One of The Top 25 Power Players in the new Hollywood" by *The Wall Street Journal*. He's contributed to the Berkeley School Of Music textbook, *The Future Of Music*. He is a frequent guest speaker on the gaming and music industry and international youth culture. Schnur is also a voting member of the National Academy of Recording Arts & Sciences and currently serves as Chairman of the Grammy Foundation.

Madden: Music to Gamers' Ears

Having helped further the musical careers of bands like Good Charlotte, OK Go, Fall Out Boy, Franz Ferdinand and 30 Seconds to Mars over the past five years, EA Trax is using its 18th game in the franchise, *Madden NFL 08*, to introduce new bands like Atreva, Datarock, Enter Shikari, and Airbourne to the masses. The in-game soundtrack for *Madden NFL 08* is the largest in the history of the franchise. It features 27 songs from acts like Queens Of The Stone Age, Daddy Yankee, Swizz Beatz, Sum 41, Mims and Ozzy Osbourne.

"Every year is a new push to introduce not just original bands, but original music," says Schnur. "We have no fear of putting Daddy Yankee together with Queens Of The Stone Age and the Bravery. We think Ozzy sounds awesome alongside Mims. Now that most hip-hop feels as if it's become mainstream disco, we think it's essential to bring in the next phase of indie lyrical expression like Brother Ali, O-Solo and Red1. Airbourne and Datarock are great new artists signed to our Artwerk label."

Yellowcard, a band that was introduced on the *Madden 04* soundtrack, debuted "Fighting" exclusively for the latest *Madden*. Last year, the band took home Best Original Song at the Spike TV VGAs (Video Game Awards) for "Lights and Sounds" on EA's *Burnout Revenge*.

"Just to have a true football lover's videogame that everybody loves, it's the best representation of the sport," said Sean Mackin of Yellowcard. "It's been a pleasure

"At the end of the day, each game franchise has to have it's own musical personality. You can't play to everyone. You have to create personalities just like radio stations used to do. It needs to be a place to discover new music and also pay homage to the property that's being discovered with it."
—Steve Schnur

working with EA dating back to 2003 when we were first on the *Madden 04* soundtrack. There have been so many listeners that might not have heard of Yellowcard except for the *Madden* soundtrack. With *Madden NFL 08* supporting our new album, *Paper Walls*, it's pretty great to have that."

Schnur said EA Trax's goal is to give unprecedented exposure to new artists, bring platinum acts to a whole new level and help define the sound of the coming year via the biggest videogame sports franchise. "In a record industry crippled by shortsighted compartmentalization, we are proud to be what radio and MTV used to be: A music fan's favorite place to discover their next favorite artist," Schnur said. "It's an annual responsibility we take very seriously and an ongoing challenge that we love."

"All of the songs from this year's *Madden* soundtrack, along with all EA game music, is now available for purchase via EA.com as part of its efforts to deliver videogame music directly to fans," Schnur point out. "A lot has changed over the decade that *Madden* has dominated the sales charts. When you look back on *Madden*, EA would find one artist that was ahead of the curve like Ludacris in the late 90s, but for the most part game soundtracks were created internally by the music guys on synthesizers."

"In the evolution of *Madden* musically

speaking, we all realized that *Madden* itself was a cultural phenomenon," said Schnur. "*Madden* represented football. It represented gameplay. It almost became a word unto itself. When I was a kid, we followed a band's every move. If they cut their hair, we cut our hair. If they wore yellow, we wore yellow. I think *Madden* has that same type of cultural impact today. The NFL is fantastic with their understanding and support of us musically."

In fact, the NFL wants the live sport to sound like the virtual sport one day, according to Schnur. In many ways, he looked at the original MTV as the inspiration for music in *Madden*. EA focused on the type of music that would have people asking, "Where can I get that song?"

"We wanted to point the season forward," said Schnur. "We want people to hear a song in a game and then three months later hear it in an NFL stadium. MTV became more than music videos in the '80s. It became a culture stamp, an identity. I think *Madden* has become that. It defines who you are. Music is such an important ingredient in defining who you are that it's just natural that we point it forward and don't just follow."

Over the past six years, there's been a sea of change in how music companies look at games. When EA Trax first launched, Schnur had to seek out every song for the *Madden* soundtrack—as well as music for other EA

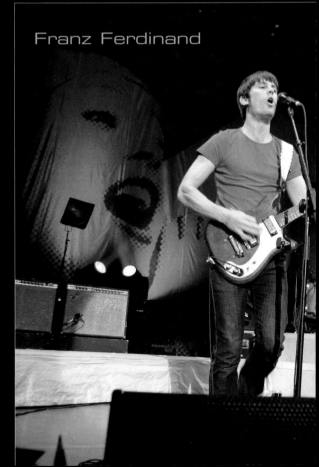

Franz Ferdinand

30 Seconds to Mars

Queens of the Stone Age

Michael Giacchino

games. He had to explain to music labels and publishers why it would be good for them to license their song to EA for the *Madden* game. Schnur said that today, radio is adding songs based on a band's inclusion in *Madden* and music video channels are creating their playlists based on the soundtrack.

"Now we have a list of about 30 songs that we choose from 5,000 song submissions from every label," said Schnur. "And every one of those 5,000 songs is fairly aggressively pitched to us. The record companies know that the videogame space is MTV-esque in its importance. They realize that to get on the *Madden* list is a feat unto itself. They know if they get on the list it will ensure that millions and millions of people will hear the band and maybe become fans of that artist. We've done a 180 in terms of how music comes to us. We have the same philosophy. We license music into *Madden* because there's a reason for every song in that game. It's our choice. People can't get that space. It's an A&R decision. We base each decision on the gamers who play *Madden* and know that one, or two, or five of those songs they're going to love."

Hollywood Composers

While EA SPORTS has helped gamers discover new music while playing, EA Trax has been busy courting Hollywood composers. In fact, Michael Giacchino, the man behind Steve Spielberg's *Medal of Honor WWI* franchise, credits that game for launching his Hollywood career. It turns out the Hollywood "It" producer J.J. Abrams, the man behind *Alias, Lost, Mission:*

Impossible III and the upcoming *Star Trek* television series, discovered Giacchino by listening to his interactive scores.

"When I started, I couldn't get a meeting with an agent or a studio or anything," said Giacchino. "Even though I had worked on videogames for Steven Spielberg, they didn't hear the word Spielberg; they heard the word videogame and thought beeps and all of these awful ear bleeding sounds. We were using symphony orchestras to create game scores, but there was such a prejudice against games in Hollywood that it was impossible to get through."

Having scored hit movies like *Ratatouille* and blockbuster TV shows like *Lost*, Giacchino no longer has a problem gaining Hollywood's ear. But he has remained close to the same gaming companies, like EA, that gave him his start. He especially likes the way EA blends interactive storytelling into franchises like *Medal of Honor*. He's just scored *Medal of Honor Airborne* for the company.

"I was amazed at the level of detail in the technology but also in the storytelling," said Giacchino. "EA had always gone to great lengths in telling great stories within their videogames. But in this one it seemed like they went further. They really do care about the story and that is not always prevalent at videogame companies. That's an area where a lot of them are still evolving."

Schnur lured award-winning Hollywood composer Mark Mothersbaugh, co-founder of '80s rock band Devo, to score the music for *The Sims 2* games. The rock composer has parlayed his avant-garde musical style into the world of entertainment where he scored, composed or directed the music for movies like *Confessions of a Teenage Drama Queen, Rugrats Go Wild, Thirteen, The Royal Tennenbaums, Rushmore,* and *Happy Gilmore.*

"Games have become very complicated, which forces you as a composer to think about music for games in a much more sophisticated way," said Mothersbaugh. "Especially with *The Sims 2,* which morphs in different ways on the whim of the player."

Schnur said this deal was a breakthrough moment in the evolution of musical composition for games. He said that now if game makers want top quality production values, they need to hire A-list talent. He added that EA holds its games to the same high standards that a major motion picture studio would claim for a blockbuster film.

"You can go places with games that you can't go with movies, TV or albums because of the technology," said Mothersbaugh. "Game consoles and PC have a regulated environment that TV, movies and radio don't, which allows us to use 3D modeling technologies invented in the 90s that don't work in other mediums."

Mothersbaugh is one of a new breed of Hollywood composers, like Giacchino, that balances musical work in both interactive and traditional entertainment. He previously worked on best-selling game franchises like *Crash Bandicoot* and *Jak & Daxter.* Mothersbaugh said that videogames offer a refreshing challenge to his steady work in films and television. He said it's nice to think about music and music composition from a different angle.

"For *The Sims 2,* I used a smaller ensemble

of 10 or 11 players on a piece," said the composer. "The schedule for this game was very similar to a movie. The music is a hybrid of an electronic and acoustic score, similar to his Wes Anderson scores, which are rhythmic and melodic."

In a relatively short time, videogame music has evolved from its "primordial inception" of bleeps and buzzes to an age where full-scale symphony orchestras record original soundtracks, said Mothersbaugh. Many of today's game publishers even release stand-alone soundtracks of videogame scores, in addition to licensed music soundtracks.

What's Next

As far as music in games has evolved over the past 25 years within EA, the future looks brighter than ever. Thanks to the current generation of always-on, broadband-connected consoles like the PlayStation 3, Xbox 360 and Wii, gamers will soon be able to interact with music in a whole new way.

"Next gen is going to provide us with the greatest highway, musically speaking, ever," said Schnur. "For years I've been promising record companies that in the future you're going to be able to hear a song in a game, click and boom—you can download it. Maybe you'll get correspondence that the band that you've been playing a lot for your touchdown song is going to be in town and, boom! You can buy tickets. Whatever the case may be, it's extremely exciting that you can continue to customize through community."

The music industry is now powered by

"In a record industry crippled by shortsighted compartmentalization we are proud to be what radio and MTV used to be: A music fan's favorite place to discover his next favorite artist."
-Steve Schnur

digital delivery as a whole generation of consumers, most of whom are also gamers, buy their music from iTunes, MSN, and other music sites. EA jumped into this market earlier in 2007, offering original music and licensed music for sale to gamers through the EA Music Store (www.ea.com/eatrax).

Gamers can purchase open-source music (the rights to which are owned by EA) and listen to the music on their PCs, MP3 players or cell phones. This list of music is constantly expanding, both with backward catalog content and as new games are released. Also through the Web site, EA also is offering a large playlist of exclusive mixes, non-album cuts and previously unavailable international tracks for sale on iTunes.com.

Gamers can buy songs like Snoop Dogg's remix of the Doors' *Riders on the Storm* from *Need for Speed Underground 2*, Lily Allen's song *Smile* in Simlish from *The Sims 2 Seasons*, Paul Oakenfold's exclusive song *Beautiful Goal* from *FIFA 07*, Spider Loc's exclusive remix of *When I Get Angry* from *Madden NFL 06*, Chamillionare's exclusive remix of *Grind Time* from *NBA Live 06*, and NFL Films music remixes. This generation of digital consumers still needs guidance, according to Schnur.

"No matter what the technology, recommendation is key," said Schnur. "There are millions and millions of songs out there. If fans feel that the people who program *Madden* and other EA songs are reliable, then we can create a 24/7 relationship with them and continue to recommend songs.

One new band we put in *Madden NFL 2003* was named Avenge Sevenfold. They sold one million songs last year. A lot of kids getting Avenge Sevenfold tattoos from hearing this band in *Madden*. That's a great way to measure success."

EA is also laying the groundwork for the next level of music and games interaction. Schnur said the next leap, which he hopes will come within a year, will be for gamers to be able to download their own songs into games and have it become a part of that world, just like the cheering crowd in a *Madden* game.

"This is a big step toward the console being the center of your living room," Schnur said. "We want to ensure that when that does, musically speaking, it's not as silly as laying a song on top of a game. Until we can achieve that, we can't guarantee consumer satisfaction." ●

Years XVI-XX: Leadership
EA Successfully Navigates Console Wars

With PlayStation sales soaring and the new Nintendo 64 flourishing as well, 1997 would be a huge year for EA. As the late 1990s wound down, EA was making changes in the office, acquiring new game-publishing talent, and pushing past $1 billion in sales.

As EA's growth continued to soar with Larry Probst at the helm, some new faces would be added at the top and old ones would find new roles. The mild restructuring of 1997 would pay big dividends in both the short and long term.

Bing Gordon, who had been with EA since 1982 and provided a lot of the early marketing vision, was named chief creative officer. New arrivals included President and chief operating officer John Riccitiello, who, with distribution and marketing in his background, would prove to be a key hire in many ways.

With sales that were continually climbing and healthy financial growth, those with a vested interest in EA would be happier than ever. But perhaps more than anyone, gamers

were the biggest beneficiaries of EA's continued evolution. With the Saturn and PlayStation markets finally in full swing, developers were constantly pushing the state-of-the-art and delivering more advanced games. Although EA was not a developer at the system's release, the Nintendo 64 offered better graphics than the other two competing consoles.

While the Saturn and PlayStation were more or less sharing titles, particularly the EA SPORTS offerings, N64 owners were constantly getting system-specific versions of popular titles. While PlayStation, Saturn and PC gamers all got an updated game with *Madden '98*, the new system got *Madden 64*. Although it featured gameplay experience to the others, *Madden 64* got a complete graphical remake. Although the commentary from Madden and Pat Summerall were somewhat limited by the system's capabilities, the lush visuals made for one of the more popular *Madden* experiences.

College football fans were treated to a new gaming experience with *College Football '98*, which ran on the same game engine as *Madden*. While the game found an audience, it would also be remembered as the first EA football game to take a note from other EA SPORTS offerings and feature an athlete on the cover—former Florida quarterback Danny Wuerffel. This approach would soon be repeated in the *Madden* series.

As the power of game consoles improved, so too did the graphics of games. The *Madden* franchise and NBA star Michael Jordan had come a long way from their pixelized debuts in the 1980s.

"Passion, creativity, and growth are all reasons that I came here and I think all of our employees feel the same way and want to make a difference."
—John Riccitiello

FIFA '98 saw the debut of a new game engine that helped make the game an international sensation.

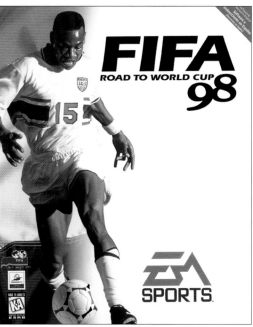

FIFA Soccer was again the most popular EA franchise worldwide. *FIFA '98: Road to the World Cup* featured an updated engine, a full soundtrack, 11 international leagues, 189 club teams, and every FIFA-registered national soccer team. An ambitiously deep title, the game set the benchmark for FIFA games to come. For fans of the simulation experience, *FIFA Soccer Manager* provided a glimpse into the future as the robust front office feature eventually made its way to all of EA SPORTS titles.

PlayStation fans played the final episode of the popular *Strike* series in 1997, *Nuclear Strike*. While an N64 port was released, the PlayStation version was more detailed, with longer missions and dynamic cut scenes.

Racing fans got a pack of fresh releases in 1997. The *Need for Speed* series had its first big hit in 1997 with *Need For Speed II*. Departing from the realistic approach of its predecessor, the sequel provided an arcade racing experience with extensive car tuning. A forerunner of the series that followed, *Need for Speed II* set the franchise on a course that is still followed today.

Stock cars were also represented by EA for the first time in 1997. *NASCAR '98* faithfully recreated the NASCAR Winston Cup experience, featured 24 real drivers, 16 tracks, and an interactive pit stop menu. Still regarded as one of the best of the series, *NASCAR '98* also featured a full soundtrack of Southern rock music.

For fans of two-wheeled action, *Moto Racer* provided both motocross and superbike

action. With a variety of custom bikes and options, the game was a fast-seller.

EA would also branch into the world of Hollywood for the first time in 1997. With improved graphical capabilities allowing for more realism, the big Hollywood studios were looking to publish richer movie-based games. EA teamed up with Dreamworks Interactive for the first such title, *The Lost World: Jurassic Park*, an adventure game based on the movie.

By now EA was becoming more platform-agnostic, and also had launched several PC games in 1997. Having purchased popular game development studio Maxis, EA would soon begin developing a whole new genre of games. *Civilization* creator Sid Meier developed *Gettysburg!*, a real-time strategy encounter. Winning several awards and lauded for its authenticity even down to uniforms and weapons, *Gettysburg!* was an instant classic. It also offered a feature that was quickly gaining popularity: online multiplayer play. While EA recognized the appeal of this concept, another PC game served as the incubator for online gaming.

EA's adaptation of *The Lost World: Jurassic Park* was its first major Hollywood title.

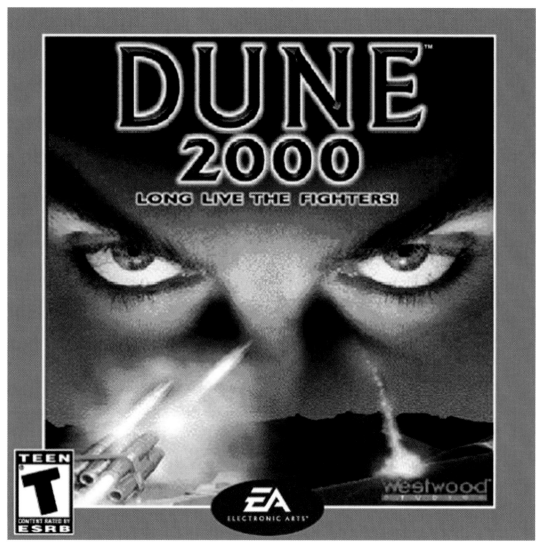

Set in the future, *Dune 2000* used the incredibly successful engine seen in *Command & Conquer: Red Alert*.

While other titles offered a one-on-one or even several-player online experience, it was *Ultima: Online* that first introduced gamers to the term Massively Multiplayer. An expensive and risky project at the time, critics felt there was no way the market would support a game that would be exclusively played by online subscribers. While the game took several years to blossom in the market (its popularity would not peak until 2003), it was truly innovative and included features like the ability to buy and customize property within the game. The game eventually became a success with over 1 million total accounts created and even today is still kept fresh with constant upgrades and updates. The latest expansion pack for the game was released in 2007.

After churning out hit after hit in 1997, 1998 would be even bigger for EA. The company had never been healthier, and growth had been steady since 1996. Although Sega's Saturn was lagging in sales, the Nintendo 64 and Sony PlayStation were quickly becoming obligatory household items for many Americans. With valuable programming experience already under their belts and the next generation of consoles still a few years off in the distance, EA was poised for more growth in 1998.

Continuing the trend of publishing games for affiliated developers, EA released the latest real-time strategy title from Westwood Studios. Based on the *Command & Conquer: Red Alert* engine, *Dune 2000* was set in the future but was essentially a retelling of the *Dune II* story. The game featured a new and improved engine, and sold well for both Windows-based computers

and the PlayStation.

In a banner year for real-time strategy and tactics games, perhaps none was more realistic in its combat than *Fleet Command*. Based on an actual Navy simulator, *Fleet Command* brought the sea aspect of warfare to life. With no management of resources or labor allocation system, the real-time tactics simulator was a draw for many simulation fans. Sid Meier also developed *Antietam!*, a sequel to his hit Civil War simulation *Gettysburg!*.

The *Populous* series was updated in 1998 with *The Beginning*. Putting players in the role of a tribe-leading shaman instead of a god for

the first time, *The Beginning* took players on an all-new quest through a fully 3D world.

Pioneering the 3D world populated by 2D sprites, *Warhammer: Dark Omen* allowed player units to develop and gain experience between missions, a first for the genre. Utilizing real-world tactics and strategies in a fictional world, *Warhammer: Dark Omen* was another real-time strategy hit for EA.

Meanwhile, Windows gamers were drawn to *Dungeon Keeper*. A notable title for its twists on the real-time strategy genre, the game marked the return of developer Peter Molyneux, who demonstrated his creative

Nearly every series was getting the 3D treatment by the late 1990s, evidenced here with *Populous: The Beginning*.

Police made their return to the *Need for Speed* series in *Hot Pursuit*, one of the most popular titles to bear the *Need for Speed* brand.

genius once again. As opposed to storming a dungeon and fighting monsters to save the day, the game put players into a world where they created the monsters and laid the traps in hopes of fending off the heroes.

Another innovative title was spun-off from an old series. Although the *Strike* titles had been popular, EA brought the series to a logical end. But it resurrected the format in *Future Cop: LAPD*. With missions ranging all over L.A. involving the X1-Alpha robot, the title paid homage to its predecessors with hovercraft and helicopters playing a crucial role.

The *Sims* titles continued to evolve in 1998, but not with another *SimCity* title. *SimSafari* took gamers in a new direction, tasking them with creating and running an African safari park. Taking all aspects of managing a park into account, (including guest happiness,) *SimSafari* led the idea of a *Sim* game into a whole new world of possibilities.

The *Need for Speed* series attained AAA status in 1998. The third title in the series, *Hot Pursuit*, brought police chases back to the game with a vengeance. Already one of the best-looking and fastest racing games around, *Hot Pursuit* took the sports-car racing title to new heights. Featuring tenacious AI, cops would try to box in players during their races, set up roadblocks, or even lay down spike strips. Turning the tables, gamers could also flip around and play the role of the police, racing in an effort to stop a six-player race before it ended.

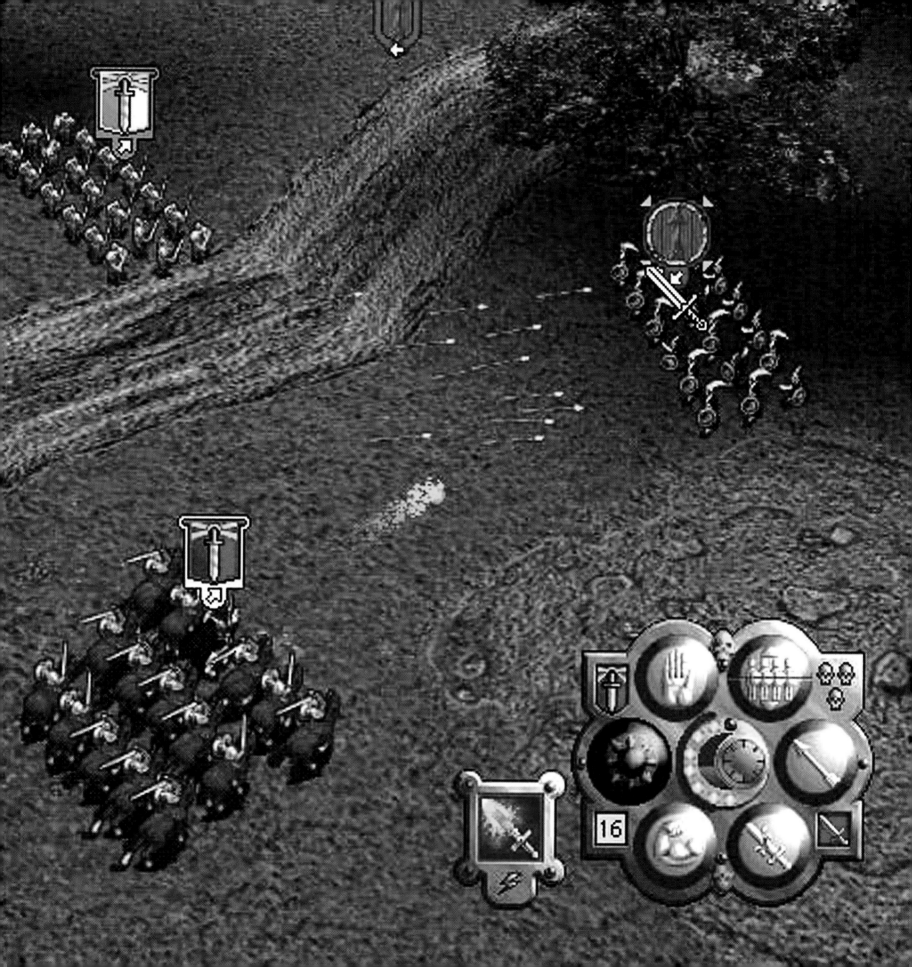

The *PGA Tour* series had been popular with golf fans, but the addition of Tiger Woods and his brand to the '99 edition made golf a signature sport for EA SPORTS.

Thanks to the easy ability to add cars and other features to the game, *Hot Pursuit* quickly developed a strong online community of fans and is the truest precursor of what the series has become today.

Racing fans would get even more titles in 1998. By taking all tracks and moving them to one interconnected road system, *Road Rash 3D* was an innovative step forward. *Moto Racer 2* also gave motorcycle fans another reason to cheer in 1998.

For fans who wanted a more authentic racing simulation, EA SPORTS released *NASCAR '99*. Focusing on the tuning of a car and how it affected driving on different tracks, *NASCAR '99* featured great graphics engine and an emphasis on simulation. With 17 tracks and a 24 car field, *NASCAR '99* gave fans the deepest racing experience yet.

EA's popular golf series got a major update in 1998. Although the heart of the game remained the same, a new name was signed-on to help promote the game: young superstar Tiger Woods. Armed with the *Tiger Woods '99* label, the golf series had the solid gameplay of its predecessors. Woods has remained attached to the title to this day, and has helped make EA's golf series into the No. 1 golf game.

Soccer fans also had reason to cheer in 1998, at least if they were playing on a PC.

1998

The *Need for Speed* series took a turn towards mega stardom as *Hot Pursuit* brought police chases back to the game with a vengeance.

AP/Wide World

World Cup '98 may not have been released until near the time of the actual tournament, but it was worth the wait to fans of the game. Taking the *FIFA* engine and turning it on its head, the 3D sports title would be the first soccer game of its kind.

Sports fans outside of North America would not be forgotten, as EA's global development began to bear fruit. *AFL '99* was released in Australia and New Zealand and quickly became a hit for its authentic Australian football experience, prompting research into a rugby title for later years. For their loyalty to the *FIFA* series, German gamers got to experience *Bundesliga '99*, a *FIFA*-based soccer game based on their domestic league. This title proved to be important, as EA's developers saw the sales benefits of localizing games to specific markets by including popular domestic leagues.

Back at home, EA released what are now annual updates for each of its EA SPORTS franchises. A new series was also introduced in 1998. With no current boxing titles on the market, EA SPORTS found a new market niche to move into with *Knockout Kings*. Featuring over 30 legends of the ring, *Knockout Kings* included a deep career mode that allowed players to develop a fighter from scratch and turn him into a championship contender.

NCAA Football '99 also gave gamers a reason to cheer. For the first time, nearly every Division 1-A football squad and their school fight songs, were featured. Including several historical teams in the mix, *NCAA*

"One of my favorite games has always been *Need for Speed* because I love the whole premise of exotic cars. It gave me an excuse to drive them and spend time thinking about what a great car simulator should be like... My favorite cars are the Ferraris. They're just an art form unto themselves."

—Don Mattrick, whose Vancouver-based studio, Distinctive Software, developed the franchise and was eventually acquired by EA

Football was finally a worthy complement to the *Madden* series.

For the first time in 1998, *Madden NFL 99* featured a franchise mode that allowed up to 30 seasons to be played. And for the last time in 1998, *Madden* would be featured on the cover of the game. In future editions, a star player would be featured on the box art.

With some of its best titles yet in 1998, strong leadership at the top, and a business plan ready for the new millennium, EA entered 1999 in dominating fashion. With a presence in over 75 countries and a direct distribution model that was fast becoming the industry standard, EA had never been more powerful.

1999 kicked off with a bang for fans of real time strategy games as the second war between the Global Defense Initiative and the Brotherhood of Nod began in *Command & Conquer: Tiberian Sun*. Featuring dynamic and malleable terrain to go along with urban cityscapes, *Tiberian Sun* included many new features, weapons, and updates.

Fans of the original *Dungeon Keeper* also got a sequel in 1999 with the aptly titled *Dungeon Keeper 2*. Although Molyneux had much less direct involvement this time, the title managed to improve upon its predecessor, most notably in terms of graphics and the "My Pet Dungeon" mode, which introduced sandbox-style gaming to the series.

Director and producer Steven Spielberg collaborated on EA's most innovative title of 1999, *Medal of Honor*. Throwing gamers back into World War II as Lieutenant Jimmy Patterson, *Medal of Honor* took authentic war sims to a whole new level. Controlling the hero from a first-person perspective,

Cinematic and action packed, the *Medal of Honor* series has brought World War II moments such as the Normandy landings of D-Day to life.

AP/Wide World

players would have to deceive, evade, and blow away Nazis.

Developed by EA at a time when movies like *Saving Private Ryan* were hitting the big screen, *Medal of Honor* was a big step in first-person shooters, ushering in the era of think-and-not-just-blast-away World War II shooters. With a sweeping cinematic score and unique levels, the game would set a lofty standard that both EA and its competitors would have to match in future releases.

Fans of the *Civilization* series had reason to be optimistic in 1999 as well when EA published the Windows version of Sid Meier's *Alpha Centauri*. Picking up where *Civilization II* left off, *Alpha Centauri* took the original turn-based strategy gameplay of the *Civilization* series to another planet.

Another major series was updated in 1999: *SimCity*. After the 1993 release of *SimCity 2000*, no other title in the series had been released until *SimCity 3000*. Not just a direct sequel, *SimCity 3000* was completely overhauled and had an entirely new feel.

One series would see its finale in 1999: *Ultima*. Nearly five years after the release of *Ultima VIII* and following the successes of *Ultima: Online*, *Ultima IX* would take the Avatar back to Britannia for one final battle. The much anticipated game would be noted for its appealing visuals and great storyline, and provided a fitting closure to the series.

EA would publish an interesting movie-related game in 1999 as well. *Warpath: Jurassic Park* did not just tap the storyline and characters from the film series, it was also a fun fighting game that featured many of the dinosaurs in the film.

Although a *Need for Speed* title was intended for the N64, gamers were instead treated to a new idea. *Beetle Adventure Racing* featured fun, arcade style driving but included just one car, the Volkswagen New Beetle. Despite this perceived lack of depth, the tracks were innovative with many shortcuts and the game was one of the best-looking titles to come out on the N64.

Fans of more realistic racing could look to one of EA SPORTS' best received NASCAR titles in 1999, *NASCAR 2000*. With updated game-

Another series that had come a long way in a short time was *NASCAR*. Soon enough, gamers would long for a version with arcade gameplay and they would be satiated with *NASCAR Thunder*.

play and many new options to mix things up, the game had just the right blend of simulation and flexibility to make it one of the best reviewed of all the *NASCAR* games to date.

For those looking for a less realistic game experience, *Need for Speed* would again deliver the goods with *Need for Speed: High Stakes*. Employing many of the features of *Hot Pursuit* along with a nice stable of exotic cars, *High Stakes* would add several new modes to the mix, like timed police pursuits and the ability to lose one's car in a chase.

Fans of EA SPORTS got the usual updates to their series, including a twist in *Madden 2000*. Barry Sanders or Dorsey Levens were featured on the cover of the title instead of just Madden, and an unnamed track that played at the start of the game was performed by an unknown rapper who called himself Ludacris.

Interestingly, *NHL 2000* and *Triple Play 2000* would feature the same play-by-play voice, with Canadian Jim Hughson calling the in-game action in both titles. *NBA Live 2000* would be notable for one man: Michael Jordan. Although he had appeared in some early EA basketball titles, he had never been featured in an *NBA Live* game. The inclusion of Jordan was even mentioned on the packaging of the game, signifying his draw to gamers.

Sports fans outside of the U.S. got a new taste of EA SPORTS' talent in 1999 with *Cricket 2000*. Taking the popular sport and applying aspects of their baseball engine to it, the title would prove to be an international success in the vein of *AFL '99*. The *FIFA* franchise was turned into three games in 1999 (one for the U.S., one for the UK, and one for Germany) but by now EA SPORTS developers recognized the need for one cohesive title.

With another big year, EA stomped into 2000 as the most powerful force in third-party game publishing. With popular titles in virtually every genre, EA was well-positioned to enter the new millennium and thrive in the upcoming round of console wars.

Sony launched their PlayStation 2 in 2000. Playing DVDs but backwards compatible to the PlayStation's games, the PS2 was instantly popular with gamers. EA was again quick on the draw and had a battery of titles ready for the new system.

Larry Probst is quick to point out the benefits of being in on the launch of the PS2. "On the PlayStation, we ended up with a market

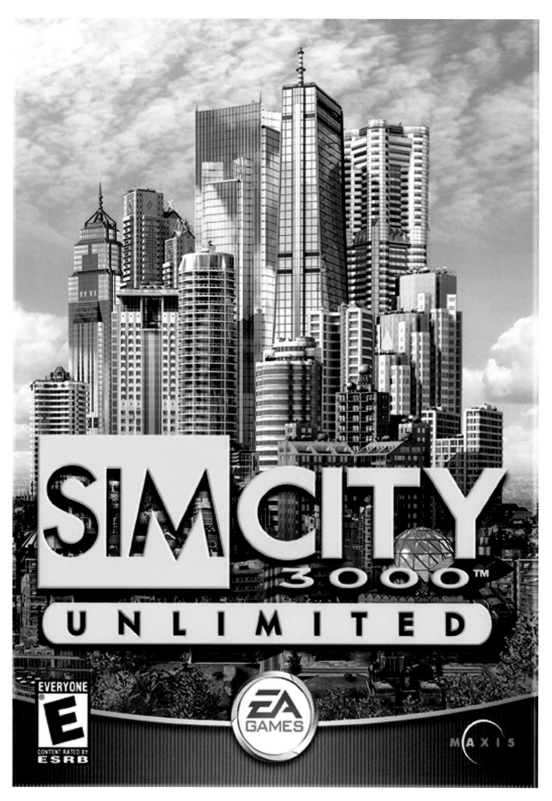

share in the high teens," he said. "At a strategic level once we started to receive information about the PlayStation 2, we set the goal to be the #1 publisher on that platform. We put ourselves in position to do that, and that really helped the company take off and become the clear leader in the industry."

EA also released a PC game in early 2000 that was one of the most original games of the new year. *American McGee's Alice* had the white rabbit drag Alice back to Wonderland, but with some macabre twists on Alice's adventures. In this innovative title, Alice would have to make use of several deadly weapons to end an evil dictatorship in Wonderland.

The popular *Command & Conquer: Red Alert* series was also updated in 2000. Focusing on a reborn Soviet Union's invasion of the U.S. from Mexico, *Red Alert 2* caused controversy due to the realistic nature of missions that involved the taking over and destruction of major U.S. landmarks.

Another Westwood title made a splash in early 2000, the RPG *Nox*. With a new slant on RPG storytelling, the game was notable because of its protagonist, Jack. A stereotyped trailer-park resident, he is sucked through a portal along with his television into the game, a first in the genre.

Showing that the PlayStation still had life left, EA was quick to release a sequel to *Medal of Honor* with *Medal of Honor: Underground*. Overlapping the cinematic story of the first game, *Underground* puts players in the role of a French Resistance fighter.

SimCity had grown from a niche title into a major PC hit, and *SimCity 3000* managed to meet gamers' expectations after the wildly successful *SimCity 2000*.

EA SPORTS slowly added faster and more extreme sports titles in the late 1990s. Boxing hit *Knockout Kings* is seen on top and EA SPORTS BIG debut game *SSX* is seen below it.

Given the strong history in the genre, it was only natural that EA publish a real-time tactics game at launch for the PS2. Kessen would take the new technology and use it to its fullest, providing the unique background of feudal Japan as its setting. For some time, it would be the only real-time war game available on the system and it was the first to take advantage of the DVD technology in the PS2.

Shogun: Total War would take the war simulation to a new level, featuring unmatched scale and depth at the time of release. It was also a huge hit with online gamers, and retains a following of players to this day.

EA SPORTS titles were well represented on the new PS2, headlined by *Madden*. The latest incarnation of the game was essentially just an updated version with new graphics for the PS2 and Eddie George was featured on the cover.

The *NASCAR* series also saw its annual update in *NASCAR 2001*, but it was a spinoff game that garnered all the attention of NASCAR fans. The arcade-feel of *NASCAR Thunder* would take the stock cars of NASCAR and place them on crazy tracks with power ups, providing interesting updates to a game that some said had gone stale.

Racing fans saw another unique title from EA in 2000 with *Need for Speed: Porsche Unleashed*. Taking the feel of racing from the previous games and applying it to cars strictly of the German manufacturer, *Porsche Unleashed* provided a deep, if specific, selection of cars

and a more realistic racing experience. Another innovative racing title that drove out of the garage in 2000 was *007 Racing*. Putting gamers behind the wheel of some of James Bond's favorite rides, *007 Racing* placed a premium on the use of Q gadgets, which were used to destroy other vehicles on the tracks.

EA SPORTS officially entered the extreme sports genre with its new EA SPORTS BIG label in 2001. *SSX*, an arcade-style snowboarding game, was the first title released under the new banner. With great gameplay, mind-boggling trick possibilities and cool tracks, *SSX* was widely regarded as the best representation of the fast-growing sport.

But the biggest hit in 2000 came from a veteran EA developer who had dramatically scaled down his broader approach to pre-

EA SPORTS' games and graphics would blossom on the PS2, Xbox, and GameCube.

NBA Street helped to give EA SPORTS BIG a footprint in the company's game portfolio. It sparked multiple sequels including NFL Street and FIFA Street.

on older demolition derby games like *Twisted Metal*, the title featured a unique physics engine that did not seek to replicate those of the real world, but instead reflect those of the cartoon world in which the game takes place.

Cartoons remained at the forefront when EA launched *The Simpsons Road Rage*, which put America's favorite cartoon family into a crazy driving game taking place throughout Springfield.

James Bond made an appearance on all three next generation consoles in 2001 with *James Bond 007: Agent Under Fire*. Featuring a storyline that did not overlap with any of the Bond movies, the game still managed to capture an audience for its depth and storytelling. As had been the case since *GoldenEye*, *Agent Under Fire* also featured a full multiplayer mode, bringing the Bond-themed death match into the 21st century.

One of the most innovative titles in 2001 was a PC-only release: With Peter Molyneux again leading design, *Black & White* offered players a new twist on god games. Players tried to grow their congregations throughout the in-game world while a battle of gods swirled overhead.

Dreamworks was quick to collaborate on another title with EA, this time in a game called *Clive Barker's Undying*. Although featuring the normal perspective of a first-person shooter, the game includes several RPG elements, including its story line and the ability to use spells to defeat the undead.

Although not developed by EA, the company published *Quake III Revolution* for the PS2 in 2001. While lacking online play, EA made

vious simulation titles. By starting out players with just a person and a house, EA's release of Will Wright's *The Sims* (Also see the *Sims* mini-chapter) was pure genius.

With robust sales in 2000 and the successful launch of the PS2, EA continued to build on its successes. As *The Sims* began to take off, EA could see a new market developing where games could be highly personalized by individual players.

Entering 2001, EA started turning some of these ideas into reality just as two new consoles, Nintendo's GameCube and Microsoft's Xbox, entered the fray.

One of the first titles for the new systems would be a spoof on demolition derby-type games, *Cel Damage*. Taking a whimsical slant several changes to the *Quake III Team Arena* engine and had another hit on its hands.

Featuring a third-person perspective, *Max Payne* was also a big shooter title for EA in 2001. With major cinematic influences that drew parallels to the *Matrix* series of movies, *Max Payne* featured slow-motion battles and gunfights. With a focus on shooting, and its Wachowski-like cinematography, *Max Payne* was critically acclaimed and sparked a sequel.

Taking the cinematic experience to a new level, popular kids title *Harry Potter and the Sorcerer's Stone* was released on every major platform in 2001. Closely following the book that preceded it and the movie that would follow it, *Sorcerer's Stone* occupied a unique niche in the *Happy Potter* story arc.

NBA Street was launched under the EA SPORTS BIG label in 2001. While some pundits felt the *NBA Live* series had gone stale, EA took traditional 5-on-5 basketball and turned it into a playground masterpiece that brought a fun, arcade feel to the game.

Football and soccer versions would follow, but *NBA Street* best symbolized EA's arcade-style sports offerings in 2001.

The *NHL* series would see its first major overhaul in over three years with *NHL 2002*. New graphics, a new engine and new commentary were all included. Also updated for the new systems, *Madden NFL 2002* featured an overhauled graphics engine that included smoother animation and new player models.

With ever more innovative titles resonating with an expanding market, Frank Gibeau acknowledges one of EA's major strengths. "I think we excel at pushing creative boundaries. There is way more creative stuff going on in this company than anybody

would ever expect," he said.

As EA got more proficient at developing games that made the most of the latest technology available, realism became increasingly important in games. After 20 years of making games, the pixels had finally shrunk enough so that a casual observer could walk by a screen and be fooled into thinking players or vehicles in a game were real. The gap between art imitating life was shrinking, and EA was helping to squeeze it shut. ●

For years, EA had prided itself on making the most of available technology. Finally, its games were beginning to take on cinematic qualities.

EA Casual is all about reaching a new type of
gamer, one that may not be inclined to shell out the
big bucks for a PS3 or Xbox 360 title.

EA Casual Expands Demographics by Keeping it Simple

Many people may forget that Electronic Arts was actually founded on the basis of casual PC games like *Hard Hat Mack* (a derivation of Nintendo's *Donkey Kong*), *Archon* (an expansion of *Chess*) and *Pinball Construction Set* (which brought the popular arcade pastime home). Even its lucrative EA SPORTS franchises like *Madden NFL, NCAA Football, NBA Live* and *NHL* spring from games aimed at the casual gaming market.

There's been a paradigm shift in the videogame industry over the past few years, thanks to the success of EA's own *The Sims* franchise, the popularity of Nintendo's Wii and Nintendo DS systems, the proliferation of casual online gaming through sites like EA's Pogo.com and the explosion of mobile gaming on devices like mobile phones and iPods. Electronic Arts has made an effort to lead the market in this new casual space, which targets gamers of all ages and types, by creating the EA Casual label and appointing Kathy Vrabeck president to oversee all facets of this emerging business.

"I think what [EA CEO] John Riccitiello recognized was that this is a business that needs to be run differently than the rest of the businesses, if it's going to capitalize on the kind of growth that people are talking about in the casual gaming space," said Vrabeck.

"I'm not narrowing it down by traditional demographic measures: age, gender, where they live, or income. We're really looking at it as opening up interactive gaming to people."

An EA Casual label won't be on the boxes of games. In fact, consumers will never even know this initiative exists within the company. Vrabeck said EA Casual is about people who are looking to be entertained in some sort of gaming format in short bursts of time, whether that be a game of on Pogo.com or *Tetris* on an iPod or a quick game of EA Playground on Nintendo Wii.

"It doesn't mean they won't sit down and play for three hours, but the game experience gets right to the fun," said Vrabeck. "It's important to provide early rewards and continue to reward players often for their play. It's about making it easy to access a game, which doesn't mean charging $60 for an Xbox 360 or PlayStation hardcore game."

PCCD

FAMILY FUN PACK — 3 MEGA-HIT GAMES IN 1!

POPPIT! To Go
Popping puzzler for everyone!

WORD WHOMP To Go
Word game excitement!

PHLINX To Go
Action-puzzle adventure!

EVERYONE
ESRB
CONTENT RATED BY

PC
CD-ROM
SOFTWARE

pogo.com™

"Pogo.com's games
are addictive..."
– USA Today, Mike Snider

With over 200 million potential casual gamers on the Internet, the fun-yet-simple Pogo is among the most successful casual gaming ventures.

Hasbro

EA further solidified itself in the burgeoning casual gaming market by acquiring the entire library of classic Hasbro games and children's brands for use in videogames, including *Battleship, Risk, Clue, Boggle, Simon, Monopoly, Scrabble, Yahtzee, Tonka* and *Littlest Pet Shop*. The deal, which extends through 2013 with the option for four additional years, brings the most recognizable casual board games to EA, which has the potential to use them online for Pogo.com, through mobile phones with EA Mobile and through PC, console and handheld games. In addition, the PlayStation Store and Xbox Live Marketplace are ripe playgrounds for Hasbro titles. If you look at the Wii, it is a perfect platform for gamers young and old to congregate around the TV and play new versions of classic games.

"The gaming market has never been more primed for a revolution in how families enjoy games," said Vrabeck, "Hasbro is the ideal partner to help propel this change. These are games that we all love and remember from our childhoods."

With the first games expected to hit the market in 2008, this deal also serves as a window for EA's own brands to expand to traditional toys and board games. Hasbro will bring some of EA's games to toy stores, which gives EA the potential to reach a new, younger audience.

EA veteran executive Chip Lange, who oversees the Hasbro brands, said this deal is part of the overall company initiative to expand the gaming market beyond the traditional 18 to 34-year-old gamer. The fact that families are familiar with the Hasbro brands and that the games themselves are easy to learn, opens the door for both older and younger audiences to try EA's digital incarnations of these titles.

Pogo.com

According to comScore, over 200 million people play casual games online worldwide. In the U.S., over 60 million people, a third of the online population, play online games at least once a month. In Europe, over 40 million consumers play online casual games: in certain countries close to half of the online population play casual games.

Pogo.com launched in 1999. It was one of the first online sites dedicated to casual games in the U.S. Today, Pogo has over 12 million monthly visitors worldwide and online sites in the U.S., United Kingdom, France and Germany. Pogo.com is the leading dedicated casual games site and accounts for close to half of all minutes spent on online games in the U.S.

Pogo grew fairly quickly in its first two years through partnerships with other online sites and by word of mouth. From the beginning, Pogo put equal emphasis on game quality and community. Players had a wide selection of games, from puzzle to traditional card to board to word. Players could chat to each other in games, set up profiles and a friends list and win tokens (points) across the service.

By 2000, at the top of the Internet boom, casual games were a leading online activity with millions of consumers playing daily. In addition, these games drew a diverse, mass-market audience. There was a plethora of casual online game sites and

AP/Wide World

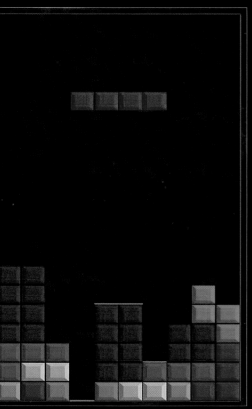

"This is a business that needs to be run differently than the rest of the EA businesses if it's going to capitalize on the kind of growth that people are talking about in the casual gaming space." —Kathy Vrabeck

most online portals had a casual games channel. As with most online business at the time, the casual games site generated revenue solely through selling advertising. The frenzy came to a halt in 2001 when the Internet bubble burst.

Many sites and portals shut down or scaled back their online games operations, as they were unable to generate revenue from their users. EA purchased Pogo.com in March 2001 for a reported $50 million.

But in 2003, the online casual games space was resuscitated. In an effort to generate revenues, companies began testing pay-to-play models. Developers and publishers began selling casual games directly to consumers online. These "downloadable" games had enhanced graphics, sounds and gameplay features. Consumers purchased the games online then played offline. Pogo took a different approach and launched an online subscription service — Club Pogo. In addition to more than 118 games available on Pogo.com, the Club Pogo service offers members exclusive games with enhanced graphics, sound and player features. Club Pogo was an instant hit and had over 300,000 subscribers within the nine months. By 2004, it was clear that consumers were willing to pay for casual games. Unlike the core videogame purchaser, the core casual game consumer proved to be female and 35 and up.

"Over the last three years, the casual games market has exploded," said Beatrice Spaine, vice president of marketing for Pogo. "Once more, there are hundreds of sites where users can play and or download casual games. Some sites are for the mass market; others attract mainly children or teens and young adults. Companies are able to monetize their audience in multiple ways through advertising, downloadable games, subscriptions and micro-transactions. The rapid increase in Internet and broadband penetration has boosted the number of people playing games online and the quality of online and downloadable games."

Pogo continues to be a leader in the space: enhancing its games offerings and features and developing new community and new revenue models. Club Pogo now has over 1.5 million paying subscribers. In late 2006, Pogo was the first major U.S. casual site to introduce micro-transactions through Pogo Gems, as well as the first to offer connected downloadable games.

"Pogo is truly a mass-market product with all major age groups [persons under age 18, 18-34, 35-49, and 50 plus] about equally represented," said Spaine. "From the tween girl to the 75 year-old retired grandfather, they all play games on Pogo. Teens and young adults typically come to pogo to take a short break in between study or work. These players tend to come less frequently and for shorter time periods. The Club Pogo subscriber is at the other extreme. Typically a woman who is 35 or older tends to play daily and on average spends more than 12 hours a week on Pogo. These older players view Pogo as a place to unwind and escape. Pogo players over age 50 also state that they play casual games to keep their minds sharp."

With its strong community aspect, Pogo.com players have formed thousands of relationships that range from friendships to marriages to support groups. Over 70 percent of the Pogo.com audience normally play card games on Pogo.com, while half play word and casino games. Roughly 60 percent of the female Pogo.com audience chat while playing a game, and of those who chat, over 70 percent discuss the specific game they are playing, according to comScore.

EA Mobile

There are an estimated 1 billion mobile handsets in circulation worldwide, of which 85 percent are game enabled. It's a breathtaking opportunity with new markets and great new games to be played on a broad array of equipment. Although EA wasn't the first game publisher to make the plunge into mobile — the company licensed out its brands early on through other game makers — when it did make the plunge, it was huge.

The reported $680 million acquisition of mobile phone game publisher JAMDAT Mobile in February of 2006 catapulted EA into the leading global position as a mobile phone game publisher. The prescient purchase also served to validate the importance of the mobile phone as a gaming platform at a time when the market was just emerging. EA recognized that mobile phone gaming was

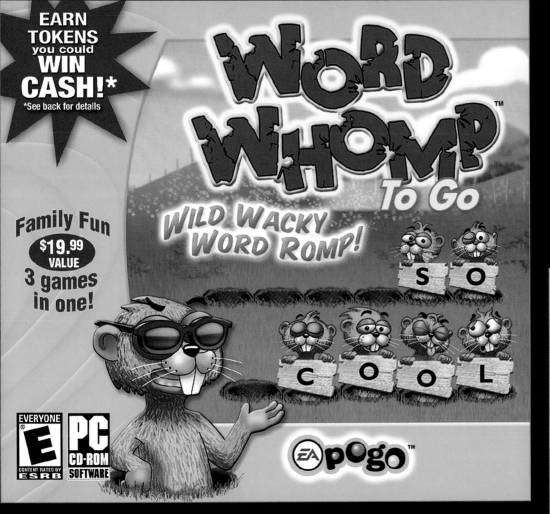

Family Fun
$19.99
VALUE
3 games
in one!

WORD WHOMP™
To Go
WILD WACKY WORD ROMP!

SO SO

C COOL L

EVERYONE
E
CONTENT RATED BY
ESRB

PC
CD-ROM
SOFTWARE

EA pogo™

Super Pop!
+20 bonus

UNDO   42   NEW GAME

The latest generation of Pogo games feature enhanced graphics, sound, special features and are playable offline.

pogo.com™

Tumble Bees
To Go

A honey of a spelling game!

EVERYONE
E
PC
CD-ROM

Poppit! To Go
pure puzzle popping pleasure!

pogo.com™

One of nearly 120 Pogo games available, the addicting puzzler *Poppit!* Is one of the most popular.

growing in popularity with consumers and that the mobile phone was rapidly becoming the most ubiquitous software delivery platform in the world. Mobile phone game publishing represented a completely unique distribution channel via the wireless carriers, and the mobile phone as a new platform for which to develop.

This acquisition enabled EA Mobile to accelerate its entry into the space by gaining access to over 100 wireless carriers, as well as proprietary development and porting capabilities from studios in Montreal, Los Angeles, Romania and India, and the No. 1 mobile intellectual property, *Tetris*. EA Mobile is now one of the main platforms within EA Casual Entertainment, and is a vital part of the growing casual gaming category for EA.

"The cell phone is the platform that is leading the way in growing the casual gaming market," said Vrabeck. "Games like *Tetris*, *Bejeweled* and *Solitaire* appeal to a broad audience and have been the defining applications on cell phones to date. Newer handsets with larger screens are enabling advanced 3D graphics as well as connected and multiplayer features; a dramatic increase from the black and white games of just a few years ago. This evolution will expand the types of games that can be offered on handsets and should attract new consumers to cell phone gaming."

"Puzzle games like *Tetris* and *Bejeweled* are perfect for this platform and resonate with mobile consumers for a variety of reasons," she said. "The games visually fit on small screens and are perfect for a simple, one-finger interface. They are easy to pick up and

play for all types of consumers, but provide a lot of value because they are difficult to master. These brands also communicate a strong value proposition to the consumer in a single line of text on the carrier deck, which contributes to its placement and therefore, popularity."

"Mobile represents an enormous addressable audience, with a global, growing consumer base," said Vrabeck. "By bringing EA's properties to mobile, we can extend EA's existing franchises to consumers who may not have played those games before. We can also provide another touch-point to a consumer who loves that franchise, but wants to enjoy it on their phone. Lastly, we believe there are a host of consumers who simply don't have the time in their lives to sit down and play a game for more than a few minutes, and mobile is a perfect casual extension of EA's consumer reach."

New technology is bringing the mobile gaming experience closer to portable systems like Nintendo DS and PSP. New 3D-enabled phones are having a positive impact on the mobile space. While 3D games may not dominate the mobile space (where puzzle games like *Tetris* and *Bejeweled* currently lead), phones that are capable of creating 3D content are generally more powerful devices that greatly improve the gameplay experience.

"Better devices will be able to provide not only new 3D games, but will also be able to supply significantly higher-quality content across the board with 3D and 2D games alike)," said Vrabeck. "We've seen this positively demonstrated with Verizon and the VCAST offering, where we have

EA wasn't the first company to provide games to mobile phone users, but with a base of over one billion handsets in circulation, mobile phones represent an attractive market.

"It doesn't mean they won't sit down and play for three hours, but the game experience gets right to the fun. It's important to provide early rewards and continue to reward players often for their play. It's about making it easy to access a game, which doesn't mean charging $60 for an Xbox 360 or PlayStation hardcore game." —Kathy Vrabeck

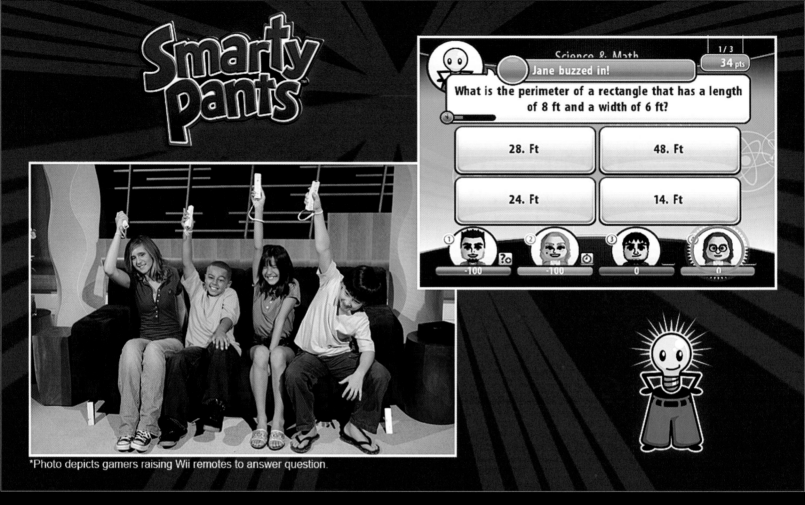

Smarty pants

Science & Math 1/3 34 pts

Jane buzzed in!

What is the perimeter of a rectangle that has a length of 8 ft and a width of 6 ft?

| 28. Ft | 48. Ft |
| 24. Ft | 14. Ft |

① -100   ② -100   ③ 0   ④ 0

*Photo depicts gamers raising Wii remotes to answer question.

---

used VCAST devices for a 3D version of *Madden*, as well as a significantly upgraded multiplayer and chat version of *Tetris*."

In 2006, EA Mobile deployed 58,000 versions of its mobile games (each handset and carrier requires unique software) to over 75 carriers worldwide. The EA Mobile portfolio of franchises includes global sports blockbusters from its EA SPORTS brand like *Madden NFL 08*, *FIFA Soccer 08* and *NASCAR 08*, as well as original EA properties like *Need for Speed* and *The Sims*, and casual games like *Tetris*, *Bejeweled*, *Scrabble* and *Pictionary*.

The EA Mobile headquarters are located in Los Angeles, but the division also holds operations in Montreal, Canada (Studio and Deployment), London, England (EA Mobile Europe Headquarters), Bucharest, Romania (Deployment, Q/A Testing and Product Development), Hyderabad, India (Deployment), Tokyo, Japan (Sales and Marketing) and Hong Kong, China (Sales and Marketing).

Casual Integration

Beyond Pogo.com and EA Mobile, EA is integrating casual gameplay into many of its titles. One such example is the entire lineup of EA SPORTS Wii games for this year. *Madden NFL 08*, *FIFA 08* and *NBA Live 08* all include a new Family Play feature that's been designed to take advantage of the diverse age demographic of Nintendo gamers. Any parent who's attempted to play a kid at a videogame knows that the younger you are, the better you are at games. It's a hand-eye coordination thing, which, unfortunately, can make playing cross-generational games a blowout.

Each of the new Wii EA SPORTS games offers an Advanced or Family Play option for gameplay. A grandparent or parent can pick Family Play and their grandchild or child can pick Advanced in the same contest. What this means on the virtual playing field is that artificial intelligence will control almost every aspect of the game for the older gamer, while the youngster will be controlling everything — as is normal with a game. Family Play essentially unplugs the Nunchuck controller from the Remote controller and just focuses on the fun motion-sensor stuff like kicking or throwing the ball.

Anyone who's played a sports game, especially *Madden NFL 08*, on an Xbox 360 or PlayStation 3 knows how complicated the game has become as it has strived for more realism. This has left out a large audience of intimidated and lapsed gamers. The new Wii game opens them back into the fold. But the casual aspect of gaming has also been implemented in Xbox 360 and PS3 games like *Burnout Paradise*. The next generation racer has eliminated all of the traditional obstacles like waiting rooms and level loads to allow gamers to immediately jump into the online action seamlessly. The game has been designed for anyone to play and offers a deep experience for the more veteran players as well as the ability for novices to get straight to the action with no waiting.

There are currently over 168 million Americans playing games and that number

AP/Wide World

has been increasing exponentially through online, mobile, new console and portable offerings in the space. EA Casual is building on the future of the $30 billion videogame industry. While the core gamers and early adopters will continue to be the backbone of the industry, the future of games is in the casual space. There are literally billions of untapped gamers out there to attract and EA has positioned itself, through its sports games and strong intellectual properties like *The Sims*, *Tetris* and Pogo, to be at the forefront of this new frontier. ●

The EA Casual label promises to open up gaming to a wider demographic than ever before.

Years XXI-XXV: Collaboration
A 21st Century Pop Culture Powerhouse Emerges

With 2002 being the first year of a three-year span with no updates in console technology, and therefore no new hardware learning curve to deal with, EA's programmers and game artists could focus on simply making great games.

It was a good year for PC gamers as well, as EA published a strong lineup of titles. *Freedom Force*, which involved defending fictional Patriot City with a band of superheroes, was the most unique. An homage to the golden era of comic books, the real-time tactics/role-playing game was a surprise hit.

Two fresh incarnations of the popular and critically acclaimed *Medal of Honor* series were released: one for PC and one for the console. While PS2 owners got their fix with *Frontline*, PC gamers were astounded by *Allied Assault*.

The first game of the series to come to the PC, and to date the only PC-exclusive *Medal of Honor* title, *Allied Assault* takes World War II infantry action to Europe and North Africa. With a multiplayer mode that supported up to 64 players at once, Allied Assault was a solid foray onto the PC for the series.

Meanwhile, *Frontline* put gamers on Omaha Beach during D-Day, and the multi-sensory experience is among the most riveting videogame levels ever created. Even John Riccitiello is a fan, agreeing that "getting off Omaha beach was an unbelievably hard challenge."

PC gamers and WWII buffs would rejoice later in the year when a second World War II title, *Battlefield 1942*, launched. Taking a markedly different approach than the *Medal of Honor* series, *Battlefield 1942* featured a more macro, cooperative focus and the ability to pilot craft as large as Navy vessels and Air Force bombers.

There was yet another big shooter released on PC in 2002, this time thanks to Westwood Studios: Taking place during the events of the first game of the series, *Command & Conquer: Renegade* took C&C outside the realm of real-time strategy for the first time.

Burnout 2: Point of Impact was one of the more notable racing titles of 2002, and the Crash Mode, which was a single contest to see how much damage a player could cause

Battlefield 1942 was a bigger and more expansive WWII experience than the Medal of Honor games.

With no new hardware on the market in 2002, the brains at EA could focus on simply making great games.

Racing titles have been historically strong for EA, encompassing a broad array of motorsports. From realistic F1 simulations to crazy motocross racing and everything in between, racing fans have long been able to burn virtual rubber.

to his car, was especially popular with fans.

The NASCAR nation got its fix in 2002 with *NASCAR Thunder 2003*, notable for its expanded career mode. Featuring a much deeper approach to the *NASCAR* simulation, the game actually requires players to coordinate their pit crew and sponsorships in the game, a first. International racing fans also got a taste of the good life with *F1 2003*. Motocross fans would not be ignored either, as *Freekstyle* was released for the GameCube and PS2.

Although it was not the deepest of games in the series, *Need for Speed: Hot Pursuit 2* brought another of EA's flagship franchises to the new generation of consoles. With exceptional graphics, the game focused on fun gameplay and brought back the popular Hot Pursuit mode where players could competing as the police.

In 2002, EA SPORTS' flagship franchise *Madden NFL 2003* hit the gridiron and featured a rudimentary online gaming mode in its PS2 version. Played on EA SPORTS servers, this groundbreaking element for the series marked the incarnation of the wildly successful *Madden* Online mode.

Two other sports titles got new graphics engines in 2002 as well. International bestseller *FIFA 2003* garnered rave reviews for its updated game engine, which allowed for unsurpassed control. *NHL 2003* also hit hard, and despite gameplay that was more arcade than simulation, the game won rave reviews for its overhauled engine and neat

According to the NPD Group, EA's *Madden NFL 2004* sold more than this many copies in 2003:

3,770,000

features like goal replays, which synced-up music from the game's soundtrack to go with slow-motion replays.

With the popularity of Will Wright's *The Sims* soaring to greater and greater heights, Sid Meier's *SimGolf* hit the PC market in 2002 and gave the *Sim*-series another hit title. Tasking players with creating and playing of golf courses, the title provided a surprisingly deep experience while retaining the wit of *The Sims* line of games.

As 2002 came to a close, EA launched one of the most critically acclaimed games of the year based on a movie. Featuring nine minutes of never-seen movie footage, *The Lord of the Rings: The Two Towers* was notable for its seamless transitions between the movie footage and gameplay. It earned several awards and topped most console best-seller lists.

After yet another successful year, 2003 started with a bang: *Command & Conquer: Generals* used a new engine based upon *Renegade* from the previous year and gave players all new factions to choose from. Although some fans of the series were skeptical of a game that departed from the GDI/Nod and Allies/Soviet storylines, the game was a big step forward and earned favorable reviews.

Among the best-selling titles of 2003 would be another sequel: *SimCity 4*. With vast improvements over *SimCity 3000*, the game featured a new regional focus and allowed players to drop their *Sims* into their city and have them report back to the player with feedback on his city.

Meanwhile the *Medal of Honor* series shifted to the Pacific Theater in 2003 with *Rising Sun*.

NBA Street Vol. 2 brought many legends of the game back to the playground. LA Laker great James Worthy is seen going vertical here.

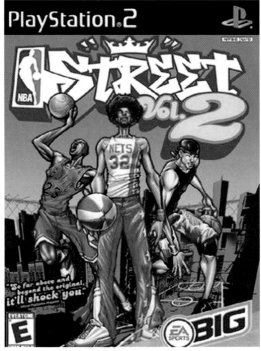

Starting with a thrilling escape from Pearl Harbor, *Rising Sun* expanded EA's WWII franchise and was notable for its award-winning soundtrack.

Taking place in a fictional alternate U.S., *Freedom Fighters* was an interesting third-person shooter that brought simple squad control to a mass-market videogame.

Need for Speed sped in a new direction in 2003 with *Underground*. Throwing players head-first into the street racing Import scene, the game featured an integrated storyline to go along with the racing and expanded the depth of the IP.

EA SPORTS BIG was back in 2003 with the release of *NBA Street 2*. Featuring new legends and game modes, the game was another big seller and led EA SPORTS BIG to contemplate an NFL release in the series.

EA SPORTS kicked in a new era of baseball gaming with *MVP Baseball 2004*. Unique in several respects, the game introduced several innovations in baseball videogames. In the Career mode, players were allowed to play with a team's minor league affiliates all the way down to the AA level, helping to manage prospects. Also, the new pitch meter placed more of a premium on defensive play.

While *NASCAR Thunder 2004* was the last game in the *Thunder* series, it included an innovative feature that was never seen before—EA SPORTS Talk. Allowing drivers to relay information via voice to their in-game crew chief, the game would even reprimand players for using profanity.

Featuring a deeper Dynasty mode than ever before, *NHL 2004* returned the series to more of a pure simulation experience. Also new was the championship cut scene: if a player was skilled enough to win the Stanley Cup, a large scale on-ice celebration would ensue, complete with the presentation and hoisting of Lord Stanley's hardware.

Madden NFL 2004 marked the 14th edition of EA SPORTS' flagship series in 2003 with the addition of a new Owner Mode. Giving players complete control over a franchise, players could make decisions as minor as hot dog prices to those as major as franchise relocation.

As games continued to grow bigger and more complex, EA proved time and again it was up to the technical challenge. After two decades in business, EA had established itself as the preeminent force in gaming. Heading into the final full year of the current generation of consoles, 2004 allowed for more new and innovative titles.

Early in 2004, *Battlefield Vietnam* was released as the first true sequel in the series. Building off the same gameplay and control points system of its predecessor, *Battlefield Vietnam* took the realism of the Vietnam War to new levels and even included granular details like booby-trap punji sticks. Years after its release, *Battlefield Vietnam* still enjoys a strong online following.

Pushing the boundaries of real-time strategy games and introducing a new style of play, *The Lord of the Rings: The Battle for Middle-earth* was really an enhancement of the *Command & Conquer: Generals* engine under the hood. Unique in its concept of a real-time strategy game based on the book and movie series, the PC game was well-received by fans and critics.

The Lord of the Rings fans who did their gaming on consoles also got a chance to

The Lord of the Rings series has been a gold mine for EA. Games based on the movies and books have been successful, and *The Battle for Middle-earth* was a strong real-time strategy title.

EA's *The Lord of the Rings* games are critically acclaimed as some of the best movie-licensed videogames ever made.

Madden has become a bona fide pop cultural phenomenon. Gamers stand in line for its annual release and the title even spawned an ESPN television series called *Madden Nation.*

bash some orcs in 2004 in *The Lord of the Rings: The Third Age.* An RPG that combined gameplay elements from several RPG franchises, the game blended them into a unique storyline not featured in the books or movies.

Medal of Honor was updated again in 2004 with the PC-only release of *Medal of Honor: Pacific Assault.* Gamers stepped in the role of a private and had to play through six intense campaigns that stretched from Pearl Harbor to Tarawa.

EA revisited James Bond in 2004 with *GoldenEye: Rogue Agent.* Although the game shares its title with the popular 1997 N64 title, *Rogue Agent* was not based on the movie of the same name and pursued a completely unique storyline with characters from the movie series mixed in.

Need for Speed returned with *Underground 2* in 2004. Resuming the storyline from *Underground, Underground 2* brought back the idea of tuning cars for street races. A new Explore mode was added that allowed players to freely roam Bayview (the city in the game) and offered three SUVs to race in.

A new *Burnout* was also released in 2004. And NASCAR fans would get a completely made over game in *NASCAR 2005: Chase for the Cup.* Featuring four separate series that fall under the NASCAR banner, *Chase for the Cup* was truly a reboot of the entire series and featured a much deeper Career mode called "Fight to the Top". Starting at

NASCAR 2005: The Chase for the Cup featured an entirely new game engine and allowed for more custom options than ever before. The series has grown exponentially as NASCAR has grown in popularity.

Frank Gibeau led the EA marketing organization during a time when the annual Madden NFL game launch moved beyond being just a videogame launch and became a mass market, pop culture event.

the bottom rung in the Modified Tour, players had to win all the circuits to become Cup champion.

After a strong showing the year before, EA SPORTS tweaked their franchises (rather than overhaul them) in 2004. For example, *Madden NFL 2005* included an increased reliance on defensive play, *NCAA Football 2005* included home-field advantage, and *NHL 2005* included Open Ice Control for controlling players off the puck.

While the EA SPORTS lineup saw little change, EA SPORTS BIG hit paydirt with *NFL Street*. Taking the concepts of *NBA Street* and moving it to the gridiron, *NFL Street*

featured fun, fast gameplay and several unique arenas. Having found yet another winning formula, EA released another *NFL Street* title, *NFL Street 2*, in time for the Holidays. The game mixed the arcade action of the original with what had become EA SPORTS' standard depth and feature set.

Another new title entered the ring under the EA SPORTS banner in 2004: *Fight Night 2004*. Taking the *Knockout Kings* series and updating it, *Fight Night* offered new realism and a revamped career mode for prospective pugilists.

With the anticipated launch of Microsoft's Xbox 360 and the PS3 and Nintendo Wii on the horizon, 2005 was a transition year of sorts, but EA was determined to capitalize on the huge installed bases of the existing consoles while also preparing for the next-gen platforms.

James Bond returned in the third-person shooter *From Russia With Love*. Following the classic movie's storyline to a T, *From Russia With Love* gave fans of Bond a big reason to cheer. For the first time in over two decades, Sean Connery reprised his role as James Bond and recorded all-new dialogue for the game to go along with his likeness.

Medal of Honor returned to Europe with a vengeance in *European Assault*. Further expanding on the original storyline of the games, it even includes a level where an American Lieutenant has to travel to Stalingrad to assist the Soviets in defending the city against Nazi invasion.

Peter Molyneux was back in action on the PC gaming front with *Black & White 2*. The game built on the innovations of its predecessor and threw more real-time strategy aspects into the game. Featuring battles and resource management to go along with more typical God-game aspects, the game would, once again, sell well.

The *Battlefield* series returned with another critically-acclaimed title in 2005 with *Battlefield 2*. Throwing gamers into a modern battle with modern weapons, *Battlefield 2* takes a departure from the more historic aspects of the earlier games in the series. With a strong Internet gaming community, the game has sold nearly 3 million copies.

The EA SPORTS BIG franchise scored another goal with *FIFA Street*. Although not

(top) Peter Molyneux returned to PC games with **Black & White 2**, a bigger and more in-depth experience than the original. (bottom) **Battlefield** came to the modern realm for the first time with **Battlefield 2**.

MADDEN NFL 06

The '06 editions of *Madden* (above) and *NCAA Football* (opposite) are considered some of the best football titles EA SPORTS has ever published.

originally as well-received as the *NFL* and *NBA* predecessors, *FIFA Street* eventually gained a solid enough following to justify sequels.

Meanwhile, EA was producing some of its best games ever as the run of the current generation of consoles was winding down. *NCAA Football 06* is widely considered to be the best game in the series' history thanks to the inclusion of Race for the Heisman mode, which allows players to create a high school player, work his way through the collegiate ranks and eventually even enter the NFL Draft in *Madden*.

The current iteration of *Madden* was also

well-received. In addition to adding Superstar Mode, the passing game received a twist with Vision Control, a beacon of light that quarterbacks would use to guide their passes. But Superstar Mode, which allowed players to extend the use of their created players in activities such as giving interviews and working out, and even taking on movie roles, was the coolest new feature. A stripped down version of the game was also ready in time for the launch of the Xbox 360.

NHL 06, also considered a great title, would return the series to its roots, quite literally, in the PS2 version. As a hidden

Easter egg, *NHL 94* could be found and played in its entirety, exactly as it appeared in 1994 with teams such as the Winnipeg Jets and Quebec Nordiques making a triumphant return. The game also included a complete redesign of the create-a-player feature, absent since *NHL 2004*.

In its final year with a MLB license, *MVP Baseball 2005* was also well-received.

One of the deepest player creation features ever in an EA game was included in *NBA Street V3*, offering nearly unlimited customization options. With more custom players, teams, gamebreakers and arenas, *V3* marked a new high in the *Street* franchise.

Some features inspired by *Street* found their way into *NBA Live 06*, the first basketball title to make its way to the Xbox 360. Players can go through Dunk School, which educates them on high-flying in preparation for the Dunk Contest during All-Star weekend. The game also takes cues from *Madden* in its dynasty mode, including a deep "Training Camp".

Burnout Revenge brought classic arcade-style racing back to the forefront with new cars and racing modes, while *Need for Speed: Most Wanted* emphasized depth. Taking many of its gameplay aspects from the *Underground* series including the sandbox city, a wider array of cars were now available and the story was made deeper than ever. Additionally, the games looked spectacular on Xbox 360.

NASCAR 06 featured improvements including Total Team Control, which allowed for new synchronization between pit crew and driver. Employing a USB microphone, players could talk to characters

in the game to maximize team efficiency.

EA was now a household name and the largest third-party developer by a wide margin, but the launch of two more new consoles presented new challenges and opportunities in 2006.

Early in the year *The Lord of the Rings: The Battle for Middle-earth II* would introduce the "build anywhere" concept for the first time, allowing gamers to literally build structures anywhere. With huge battles and an involved storyline, the game was a hit in early 2006.

Although *Command & Conquer: The First Decade* did not include any new content, it was still a hit. By including every *Command & Conquer* title and expansion pack from 1995's original all the way through 2003's *Generals*,

(above) *Black* places an emphasis on modern-day combat and authentic weaponry while *Battlefield 2142* (opposite) took warfare into the future with unique weapons and creative vehicles.

The First Decade provided a neat retrospective on a now-classic franchise.

Black, a first-person shooter with emphasis on authentic firearms, also hit store shelves during the year. With real-world environmental damage and accurate bullet physics, *Black* quickly garnered a devoted fan base that enjoyed the game's explosive action.

Battlefield 2142, a futuristic update of the revered series, quickly became one of the most popular first-person shooters in the online gaming community, while EA would mine one of Hollywood's greatest films for another big new title. A large sandbox-style game, *The Godfather: The Game* seamlessly intersperses scenes from the movie in with an original storyline for the game, with several of the original actors providing voice-overs. Showcasing MobFace, the player creation model, EA continued to define the state-of-the-art in player creation features.

EA SPORTS posted another winning season in 2006 thanks to its first run releases on the new systems. Notably, *Madden, NCAA Football, NHL 07* and *FIFA* all received new engines and makeovers for the new generation. While some considered titles such as *Madden* a bit stripped down in 2005, the latest versions returned the depth and thoughtfulness that fans of EA SPORTS games had come to know and love.

Picking up where *Most Wanted* left off, *Need for Speed* returned with another strong outing in 2006 with *Carbon.* Taking the basic model of *Most Wanted,* and tweaking the graphics while expanding the story, *Carbon* provides the deepest *Need for Speed* experience so far.

With the XBOX 360, Wii, and PS3 all on

The Lord of the Rings universe has provided great background for a gaggle of EA games.

(above) *NBA Live* has come a long way from the days of *One on One*. The newest generation of game consoles provide fans with stunning graphics.
(opposite) Thanks to *The Simpsons Game* from EA, fans can now navigate an interactive Springfield.

the market, 2007 would be a year in which, more than ever before, videogames offered something for everyone.

Due to its innovative user interface and mass appeal, the Wii received some of EA's most interesting titles in 2007. *Boogie*, a dancing and karaoke game, was among the first third-party titles to make good use of its motion-based controls while *EA Playground*

included simple mini-games such as slot car racing and dodge ball that required players to get up off their couches.

EA took some fun jabs at itself with *The Simpsons Game*. Perhaps the greatest sitcom ever, EA was praised by fans for capturing the irreverence that has makes the TV show so appealing.

Two major PC titles, one a sequel and the

other the start of a trilogy, were launched in 2007. *Command & Conquer 3: Tiberium Wars* was one of the highest rated games of the entire series, while shooter fans were treated to an all-new futuristic series called *Crysis*.

Fans of *Medal of Honor* got a double dose of WWII action with two fresh titles. Released across every major platform, *Vanguard* and *Airborne* featured new gameplay styles and some pretty stunning paratrooper attacks.

By mixing elements from karaoke with new ways to interact with a game, *Rock Band* may signify a new era at EA. With peripherals that included not only guitars and microphones, but drums and bass as well, *Rock Band's* incredible multi-player capability has kept gamers rocking, and opens up all sorts of possibilities for the future. Made in conjunction with MTV and published by EA, *Rock Band* has the mojo to be EA's next great mass market franchise.

With the industry in a continuous state of flux, and Moore's Law more relevant than ever, the only constant is change. After all the innovations that EA has made in its first 25 years, what may we look for in the next 25?

Will Wright envisions a more customizable gamer experience. "The game should be able to watch you," he said. "Almost like a game designer over your shoulder kind of deciding, 'Oh, I see. You really enjoy this part. I'm going to make this part the more important aspect of the entertainment.'"

As for the company, CEO John Riccitiello has a healthy respect for the talent he leads, and is excited about the future. "We've got a collection of people that, whether I worked here or I didn't work here, would probably

include 90 out of the top 100 people I admire, and that's really unusual. I've never had that experience before and I don't expect to have it again in any other place. I think it's pretty amazing."

Electronic artists, indeed. While the tale of EA's rise from just another third-party software publisher to a 21st century pop culture powerhouse can be traced through technology, it is still the people and the passion that have made the company the industry leader that it is today. ●

(above) *Crysis* is poised to become the next big hit in first-person shooters. Many gamers have upgraded their hardware just to play the game. (left) *Rock Band* has already changed the way fans interact with music games.

EA Into the Future
EA's past, present and future leadership looks towards the next 25 years

What is your legacy at EA? What's EA's legacy after 25 years in business?

Larry Probst: "We were just one of many if you look back 20 or 25 years. There were multiple third party publishers that were larger than EA, including Konami, Capcom and Acclaim. With a lot of hard work, good strategic thinking, and strong execution, EA became the leading company in the industry. It's not an easy thing to do and everybody aspires to be number one. I think EA's legacy over this first 25 years is that we figured out how to separate ourselves from the hundred plus other companies that were on the map at the various points in time, and put ourselves in position to be the clear and acknowledged market leader.

The challenge now is to stay ahead of the competition, and continue to drive growth and profitability. The last thing you can do is become complacent. You have to keep that paranoia that Andy Grove talked about – only the paranoid survive.

This has always been a team effort. I just feel fortunate to have been part of the team for so long. We've had a lot of success along the way. We've had a lot of fun along the way. We've had some tough challenges and disappointments along the way. But all in all, it's been a pretty great ride for everyone that participated in that process."

Bing Gordon: "EA brought class to this new entertainment medium and organized and defined the premium product. EA was the first company that had customization in games. EA was really the first to commit to simulations and the first to do games for grown-ups. We expanded the possibilities of games.

When EA went public in '89, Wall Street didn't think it was possible for a videogame company to go public, so we made it possible for a lot of other companies to go public. We basically created a high-end expectation for consumers and an umbrella for financeable companies. I think Nintendo gets credit for making the mass market.

We have this missionary slogan of 'Software worthy of the minds that use it.' I think over the past 25 years we have done that. My legacy to EA is part of that. Having worked in advertising, I'd seen that most advertising agencies had animosity between the creative side and the business side. One of the things I tried to do at EA is to create this teamwork and a relationship between the business people and the creative people. EA's still pretty good at that, and I hope that sustains."

What are the current challenges and opportunities for EA?

John Riccitiello: "We need to reach out to a much broader audience. Today, a successful game can touch as many as 20 million people. But in the years ahead we're going to see games that reach hundreds of millions of people. Getting there won't be simple but many of the big growth drivers are already falling into place.

Technology will always be a growth engine but we're also going to see advancements in the art – true character creation, empathy, more emotion. Pushing the art harder, bringing in true emotion and empathy is going to bring new audiences to gaming.

Another key to growth is lowering the barriers to entry. Today, many great games are just too hard for novices and even intermediate players to just pick up and play. Games need to be more accessible without losing the challenging levels that hard core gamers love. We have a saying at EA that helps us think through this process: 'Easy to Play, Hard to Master.' In practical terms, it means that a novice gamer should be able to have fun in the first five minutes of *Need for Speed*. But we need to design that experience without alienating the millions of people who already love the franchise for the challenging game play."

Frank Gibeau: "EA is at the dawn of a new era. We are facing new challenges in the global gaming marketplace, all of which I'd also characterize as opportunities for EA. Whether it is the diversity of our portfolio mix, the introduction of downloadable sales, developing dynamic intellectual properties that transcend the medium or growing our business in Asia, we are pushing the company and the industry forward. At EA we have the talent and ingenuity that will transform this industry."

How is the videogame business the same as other forms of entertainment media, and how is it different?

John Riccitiello: "We are an entertainment business – we have much in common with movies and other forms of media. People play games – on the PC, mobile phones, game consoles and other platforms – to have fun and relax. What makes interactive games different is the way we use

technology to put the player directly into the action, to solve the puzzle, to save the world or win the contest. The game player is brought right into the middle of the action and is often central to the story, involved in its telling. There is no other art form that engages the audience in these same ways.

> "The challenge now is to stay ahead of the competition, and continue to drive growth and profitability."
> —Larry Probst

Another point of difference is the speed of change – PC, console and handheld technology changes radically every four to five years – and when it does, it creates revolutionary improvements in how games are experienced. No other form of media embraces technology quite so quickly. Games today are vastly different from what they were just a few years ago.

What makes games like other forms of media is that at their core, games are an art form. It takes brilliant creative minds to conceive and build the products we make. It takes great care. It takes true artists."

Nancy Smith: "A relatively recent phenomenon is just how broad our demographic has gotten. That means you can create so many different types of entertainment experiences – for 8 to 80-

year-olds – I think that's terrific.

We used to build games mainly for 18 to 34-year-old males. Now we make entertainment experiences for a range of demographics, and I love that. It makes the business so much more interesting.

Gaming could have stayed a business that was mainly for teenage boys only. That could have been its destiny. I like to think that EA had a lot to do with broadening it into a major category of entertainment. I always believed from the very early days that since interactive entertainment is so engaging, I always felt confident it could beat passive entertainment.

I grew up in a family that played traditional card games and board games. To this day, I still love those games, but I was always a believer that interactive entertainment was so much more immersive and engaging and stimulating and entertaining – and now it has this great social element.

So I'm very proud of that. I think EA has led gaming to be a very broad form of entertainment. And it touches everybody today. My 75-year-old retired Mom plays Pogo three hours a day. That's very cool, and I think EA's legacy is that we made it something that was not just for that core gaming demographic that the industry serviced so heavily early on."

What does the videogames industry do a good job of, and what does it struggle with? How about EA?

John Riccitiello: "Our industry fell into a rut that we're only now getting out of. We got stuck making expensive games that appealed to a rather narrow audience, male teenagers. There are a lot of exceptions that show us the that audiences want to play new kinds of games – Pogo, *The Sims, SSX, Dance, Dance, Revolution* and *Rock Band*. For too long, our industry focused too much on sequels and games that copied other games, all seemingly designed to a formula for a narrow target audience. Today, we've got a lot of catching up to do but if we can do it, we'll be in position for perhaps the greatest opportunity our industry has ever seen.

In the past five years, a lot of technology has popped up that has really captured the imagination of the mass market like iPods and digital cameras. Others, like Myspace and Facebook, are using technology to allow consumers to maintain and build relationships. In a sense, they stole the 'wow' that was associated with games just a few years before. And, the technologies that enable instant messaging, mobile web browsing, blogging and other technology that puts the power of creation in the hands of the consumer are finding growing global markets for their products.

Games need to keep up with these trends – they need to be more accessible to new and larger audiences, and they need to foster the communities, bring together the millions of people who love games. The truth is that even our core consumers want to see it happen. There are lots of signs that core gamers aren't interested in playing sequels any longer – they want more.

EA is pressing a lot of those buttons and I think we're going to be even more exciting and culturally influential in five years than we are today. The secret is to bring new experiences to our base of consumers while we reach out to much larger audiences."

> "We need to lower the barrier of entry in picking up and playing a game. We need to be vastly more accessible...so that an average person can pick up *Need for Speed* or *Madden* and have fun in five minutes."
> —John Riccitiello

Peter Moore: "The videogame industry sets the bar for delivering incredible innovation. Games are where technology and entertainment collide, often right at the television in your living room. We do a phenomenal job of creating experiences that mediums like television, movies and music simply cannot compete with, in terms of providing control, personalization and customization.

Videogames are a multi-billion dollar industry, yet we're still establishing ourselves, in some circles, as legitimate mainstream entertainment. For all the 45-year-old men and women enjoying videogame experiences each day all over the world, there's still a larger percentage of people in that demographic who see games as a waste of time, as something primarily for adolescent males, and as toys that fuel violence and anti-social behavior.

Having spent time on the outside and now inside the walls of EA, it's clear that this company has blazed a trail that others have only been able to attempt to follow by consistently creating compelling, broad-based interactive entertainment while riding the ups and downs of technology without ever stumbling. We've innovated and been a leader for years. That's something I've always admired about EA, and EA SPORTS in particular. EA created an entire genre with the EA SPORTS brand, and when you look at how we established and then have consistently innovated in the sports category it's clear that EA SPORTS has not ridden the wave, we've driven the wave. EA SPORTS introduces fans of all ages to sports, our games help engender a love of sports, and they provide personal access to the emotion and passion of sports. That's an exciting place to be."

Kathy Vrabeck: "While the video-game industry evolves its definition of 'Casual' games, it's the consumer's definition that matters the most. The people buying casual games don't think of themselves as 'gamers', even women playing an average of 52 minutes a day on Pogo.com don't think of themselves as 'gamers'. What they want is a quick, fun and engaging entertainment experience. So while game trades write about innovation in gameplay mechanics, this consumer wants something that they can turn on and figure out how to play right away. That doesn't mean the experience is dumb-downed or shallow – if anything it can be more difficult to make something simple than it is to make it hard."

What's on the frontier for EA? And what's next for the videogames industry?

Frank Gibeau: "I think fundamentally the next frontier for the industry and for EA is operating in a connected world where gamers have a social network experience blended with their gameplay. As a company, EA will be connected to the consumer – in terms of delivering players the games, providing a community, and a fluid communication between EA, the gamer and the gamers to each other.

In addition to the closer tie between EA and our consumer, how games are played also is evolving. The Wii is showing that there is a new way to play games. It's not just banging on the controller with three buttons. The man-machine interface for interactivity is changing. That change combined with connectivity in games is altering the exchange between player and game experience, which leads to powerful new ideas for how to make games. I think we're just starting to scratch the surface on how the player lives in the game experience; making for an exciting time to be a gamer."

"I think fundamentally the next frontier for the industry and for EA is operating in a connected world – the completely connected world." —Frank Gibeau

Peter Moore: "Digitizing the business is the way of the future. At EA, we're already on the path to delivering innovative and breakthrough experiences directly to consumers at their homes and direct to their consoles, PCs or however they choose to consume games. We're already seeing the profound impact of gaming in a connected world – with sports fans from Ohio to Munich to Shanghai creating, and competing in, social gaming networks. And at EA SPORTS, we're in the enviable sweet spot where fans of sports and games can connect and compete in a place where they are speaking the global language of sport.

The next 5-10 years will see EA continuing to globalize and grasping new opportunities to grow with new business models that previously would have been completely foreign to us. We're still very much a Western company, but the tremendous promise in places like China and India allow us to think well beyond the business as we know it today."

Kathy Vrabeck: "The trend I'm most excited about is the growth in casual gamers. I've developed and marketed most game genres and enjoyed it, but I am most excited to be working to bring new games and new game players to videogames. I believe Casual entertainment is the growth vehicle for this industry. The challenge of working with a new consumer who has different gaming needs is intriguing; having the opportunity to reach this consumer as part of the #1 videogame company, is a privilege.

As part of our future, EA will make you rethink what a game is or what a casual entertainment experience is…We owe the casual consumer a high quality experience, but one which they define differently than a core gamer."

Bing Gordon: "I think it's all about the Internet. It's trying to figure out how to combine the joys of games with all the aspects of what we think of as Web 2.0, which is user-generated content, personalization and customization, interrupt ability, multi-task ability, mash-up ability of all the games.

Games have grown up and the graphics on videogames have grown up as being highly intensive session-based experiences, more like going to a movie theater. And I think the Internet is getting to be a kind of a short attention span, multi-tasking theater that mashes together creativity, communication, socialization and information. I also believe all games in five to ten years are going to take on aspects of Web 2.0.

I also believe the next thing is that videogame literacy is going to inform media advertising and education, so the kids who grow up on videogames understand the language and are motivated by the language. They like better interfaces. They like avatars. They like customization. They like scoring and tracking, user records, and multiple parallel goals. Media advertising and educators are all going to have to have aspects of videogame design in their offerings."

Will Wright: "I think gaming is very interesting for one principal reason and that games are malleable and that when you go to see *Star Wars* everybody's going to see the same version of *Star Wars*, but when you play a game, everybody's going to have a different experience, depending on what they do in the game.

Not only that, but we're getting to the point where the players can actively start changing the game with the steps they make in it or steps that other players make, and so these games have this very malleable potential already just right out of the box. And what's really interesting to me is we're starting to actually look at what the player does in a game and build player profiles to get a sense of who the player is, what they like, their skill levels, their aesthetic, what directions they would like to see the game go in, and in some sense have the game customize itself uniquely to each individual user.

The really important part, though, is that you have a way for the computer to start understanding who the player is and what they like – and then we program the game so the player enjoys it more. So after you and I've been playing the same game for a month, they might be unrecognizably different. It's almost like the skin customizes itself to the player. As an example, the game should be able to recognize after you've been playing for a few minutes if you're good or not, and it should be able to simplify itself or make itself more complex depending on your abilities and your interests. It should be able to tell by the way you're playing it whether, 'Oh, this is too complicated. I'm going to throw away some of the rules and make it a much simpler game and give you a nice, smooth ramp into the full experience,' or maybe you're totally into picking up a player lineup and you really don't care that much about running the plays, and so the game basically makes that a much more important part of the experiences and maybe the action part of the game becomes more automatic.

I've been very intrigued by that, by basically giving the players higher and higher leverage tool to create more and more aspects of the game so that they feel like they're not just kind of dropped into an environment and the back story and characters is somebody else's design. But yet, we give them as much of that creative process as possible. And so they kind of become the co-game designers."

One of the ideas behind the book is to demonstrate how EA has become an influential force in pop culture and is going to impact these more traditional media, like music, movies and television in the future. What's your take on that premise?

Will Wright: "If EA fulfills its potential, it certainly will. And it's a matter of EA broadening itself from a gaming company into an entertainment company. I think that if you look at all these other things – in some sense, gaming is a superset of all these other forms of entertainment. If people look inside of a game, you've got writing, you've got music, you've got animation, you've got actors, stories, almost anything you'll find in any other form of media, it's contained somewhere within games.

And so because of that – if there's one place where you would expect there to be kind of a central node or nexus of all these forms of entertainment, gaming would seem to be the place where you could take things into all these other directions. It could be a television show. It could be a toy. It could be a staged musical. It could be anything." ●

"When I was a teen programmer back in the 80's, I thought Electronic Arts would be the coolest company to work for. They had published many of my favorite games, like *Pinball Construction Set, Archon, One on One* and *Bard's Tale*. It was also cool that their ads put game programmers up on pedestals.

Back in the day, I sent a few submissions to EA but I had an Apple IIGS, and that just wasn't a platform they were interested in. I remember at one point saying something along the lines of "Tell me what you want to see, I can do anything!". I was advised to look at the Amiga.

A small company called Softdisk actually wanted the old 8 bit Apple II games I created and that turned out to be my entry into the games industry. My programming moved from the Apple II to the PC, and from RPGs to action games. I left Softdisk with some new friends to found id Software, and we made our mark defining the first person shooter genre of games with *Wolfenstein, Doom* and *Quake*.

Fast forward twenty years later. I took a little detour from the high end first person shooter world to see what I could do on a mobile phone. The platform required a re-thinking of core gameplay ideas. The direction I settled on was a blend of my experience with 3D rendering technology and the sense of adventure I remembered from one of the favorite games of my youth – *Bard's Tale*. That's how *DoomRPG* was born. With *DoomRPG's* success came the *Orcs & Elves* series which have been critically acclaimed and commercially successful.

Who wound up publishing them? Electronic Arts."

—John Carmack

"It truly is amazing to see what is happening with video gaming today. Animations are now so real that the line between live games on TV and videogames continues to thin. The positive connection between NBA and NBA videogames is great. Fans of NBA basketball can really get inside the game, or as EA SPORTS says it "if it's in the game, it's in the game."

We at the NBA have enjoyed our partnership with EA over the past 16 years. We consider the EA team not only great business partners, but friends. In many ways, we've grown up in sports videogames together. And, today, we are taking what we've done in the United States to China, to Europe, and to the world: bringing the fun and competition of the NBA and EA SPORTS videogames to the ever-growing legion of our shared fans around the globe."

—David Stern • NBA Commissioner

"Working with EA SPORTS we pioneered sports on videogame systems back in the 1980s. I knew we needed it to be authentic, they did that. To see what the *Madden NFL Football* game franchise looks like today, we couldn't have dreamed it would be this realistic 20 years ago when we first started out. EA has been a great partner and by working together we have created a whole new way for fans to experience and enjoy football."

—John Madden

"EA and Sony Computer Entertainment (SCE) have established one of the great creative partnerships in the history of the entertainment industry. It is a relationship that spans three systems, two decades, hundreds of games and many thousand hours of entertainment. Each time SCE developed a new generation of PlayStation, we knew we could count on our partners at EA to help connect the new technology to consumers with great games like *Madden NFL, Need for Speed, Medal of Honor* and *SSX*. So I would like to commend EA for 25 years of great partnership and great games, and to wish them the greatest success in the years ahead."

—Kazuo Hirai • President and Group Chief Executive Officer, Sony Computer Entertainment, Inc.

"Great creative minds helped Electronic Arts propel itself into becoming one of the giants in the industry. They continue to set standards for innovation and great gaming experiences, traits we greatly admire. For those reasons, Nintendo is proud to be working hand in hand with EA."

—Satoru Iwata • President Nintendo Co. Ltd.

"On the evening of May 10, 2004, I stood alongside the President of EA on the stage of the historic Los Angeles Shrine Auditorium. Together, we addressed a videogame industry audience at E3 and announced the lan mark Microsoft/EA Xbox LIVE partnership. I'll never forget it. We were framed by a wall of the world's best athletes, including boxing legend Muhammad Ali and some of the best pro and collegiate soccer, football, basketball and hockey stars. It was a seminal moment – for gamers, for EA, for Microsoft and for me personally.
EA has been a dynamic and reliable partner, and together we've delivered innovative and fun gaming experiences to consumers around the world. They are strategic in the way they think about the future of gaming and entertainment, and have a winning attitude. Like Ali and his claim that he "shook up the world" after the Sonny Liston fight, EA continues to shake up the industry."

—Robbie Bach • President, Entertainment & Devices Division • Microsoft

"A decade ago after declining to visit the EA offices in Vancouver I finally capitulated and the afternoon I spent there changed my life in many ways. The creative environment and leadership was like nothing I had experienced within the music business. Simply put EA was living its future in the "now". With EA's receptivity to making the music in the games top notch, we started an amazing journey that saw Steve Schnur enter the fold and the forming of a new copyright creative model called Artwerk insuring that we all continue living the future "now."

—Terry McBride • C.E.O. Nettwerk Music group

"We have a really collaborative creative relationship with EA, as they are just as concerned as we are to make each installment better and more exciting than the last, whilst at the same time maintaining the absolute integrity of the source material. They push the boundaries in every direction and are never happy to accept limitations in their quest for the best. They are ideal partners and we love them!"

—David Barron • Harry Potter films • Producer
—David Heyman • Harry Potter films • Producer

"So much of the cultural relevance that videogames and interactive entertainment enjoy today can be traced directly to Electronic Arts. Trip Hawkins, and the early management teams of EA believed with all of their collective heart that games were an entertainment medium for the masses. EA has had so many "firsts:" from some of the early titles like *One on One*, the first game that used licensed likenesses that fans could identify with; *M.U.L.E.*, one of the games that pioneered resource management, and online multiplay, from the late Dan Bunten; *Madden Football*; one of the great successes that tapped into consumers LOVE of football that endures to this day.
So many of the approaches, first undertaken by EA, were emulated by other publishers and developers; the list of famous alumni who have gone on to create their own game companies is a testament to how dynamic an environment they were able to create. It would take a number of paragraphs to recap the titles that have received recognition from the Academy of Interactive Arts & Sciences; their most recent win was for Burnout: Revenge. EA's original belief; risky 25 years ago, has now been validated based on how their innovative approach to the medium have helped fuel the phenomenal heights that videogames enjoy among people across the globe."

—Joseph Olin • President, Academy of Interactive Arts & Sciences